Japane
Mytho

A Fascinating Guide to the Gods, Heroes, Folklore and Traditions of Ancient Japan

Arthur Weiss

Table of Contents

Introduction

Japanese mythology is a vibrant cascade of stories woven from the threads of ancient beliefs, historical events, and cultural practices that have shaped Japanese consciousness for millennia. It is a world inhabited by gods and spirits, where heroes embark on epic journeys and supernatural beings roam the shadows.

Although these myths are ancient, their influence is far from obsolete. They continue to permeate modern Japanese culture, from traditional beliefs and religious practices to contemporary literature and art.

The purpose of this book is to discover the rich and diverse world of Japanese mythology. Through this journey, you will gain a deeper understanding of Japan's spiritual and cultural heritage and perhaps a new appreciation for the myths that have shaped one of the world's most fascinating cultures.

Welcome to the world of ancient Japan!

Chapter One: Creation Myth and the Supreme Deities

Separation of Heaven and Earth

According to ancient Japanese texts, the universe initially existed in a state of chaos, described as a formless, murky mass. This primordial chaos, often referred to as ame-tsuchi (heaven and earth), was undifferentiated and lacked any structure or order. There were no distinctions between the heavens above and the earth below; everything was intertwined in a single, undivided entity. This concept of chaos as the origin of the cosmos is not unique to Japanese mythology, but the way it is resolved into order is distinctive to the Shinto worldview.

The process of separation began with the emergence of light and sound, which gradually began to distinguish the lighter, purer elements from the heavier, impure ones. The lighter elements, characterized by clarity and brightness, ascended to form the heavens, known as Takamagahara (the High Plain of Heaven). Conversely, the heavier, denser elements descended to create the earth, known as Ashihara no Nakatsukuni (the Central Land of Reed Plains). This process marked the beginning of differentiation in the universe, establishing the spatial order that separates the divine realm of the gods from the physical world inhabited by humans and other beings.

As the heavens and earth began to take shape, a hierarchy of deities, or kami, emerged. These deities were born spontaneously from the energies that were now organized into distinct realms. The earliest kami are referred to as the Kotoamatsukami, or the "Separate Heavenly Deities." These first gods were abstract and did not possess distinct forms or personalities. They represented the initial forces that brought order to the cosmos and set the foundation for the world as it would come to be known.

The first of these deities was Ame-no-Minakanushi-no-Kami, considered the primordial god and the first to emerge from the void. This deity, often associated with the concept of divine will or universal order, is central to the creation narrative but remains largely a formless, mysterious figure. Following Ame-no-Minakanushi-no-Kami, two more deities, Takamimusubi-no-Kami and Kamimusubi-no-Kami, were born. These deities, too, were abstract and ethereal, symbolizing the fundamental forces that govern life and the natural world.

After the emergence of these initial deities, the process of creation continued with the appearance of the Kamiyo Nanayo, or the "Seven Generations of the Age of the Gods." These seven generations included pairs of male and female deities who were born from the heavens and played significant roles in the further differentiation and structuring of the world. The last pair of these deities were Izanagi and Izanami, who would later be tasked with creating the physical islands of Japan and populating the earth with life.

The separation of heaven and earth did not merely create spatial order; it also established a cosmic hierarchy and the roles of the deities within it. The heavens, being the domain of the gods, were considered the source of divine authority and the origin of the kami who would govern the natural world. Takamagahara, the high heavenly plain, became the dwelling place of the most powerful deities, including Amaterasu, the sun goddess, who would later be revered as the ancestor of the Japanese imperial family.

The earth, on the other hand, became the realm of human beings and the various spirits that inhabit the natural world. While the earth was connected to the heavens through the divine will of the gods, it was also a place where the forces of chaos could manifest, as seen in the unruly spirits and beings that would later populate the mythological landscape. This duality of order and chaos on earth reflects the Shinto belief in the need for rituals and practices to maintain harmony and balance in the world.

The separation of heaven and earth also laid the groundwork for the various interactions between the gods and humans that are central to Japanese mythology. The descent of the gods to earth, the establishment of divine rule, and the ongoing influence of the kami on the natural world all stem from this initial act of separation. It set the stage for the stories of creation, the birth of deities, and the interactions between the divine and mortal realms that would follow.

In addition to explaining the origins of the physical world, the myth of the separation of heaven and earth also carries profound spiritual significance in Shinto. It emphasizes the interconnectedness of all things, where the divine is not separate from the world but intrinsically linked to it. The kami are not distant, otherworldly beings but are present in the natural elements that make up the earth—trees, mountains, rivers, and even the very land itself. This belief in the sacredness of nature is a core tenet of Shinto and is reflected in the reverence for natural sites as places where the kami dwell.

Izanagi and Izanami: The story of the creation of the Japanese archipelago and the birth of the gods

Izanagi and Izanami are often referred to as the divine couple, and their story begins with the formation of the world. According to the Kojiki (Records of Ancient Matters) and the Nihon Shoki (Chronicles of Japan), two of the oldest and most important texts in Japanese mythology, the cosmos initially existed in a state of chaos. In this primordial void, a reed shoot emerged, and from it came the first gods, or kami. Among these early deities were Izanagi (he who invites) and Izanami (she who invites).

The divine couple was tasked with the crucial responsibility of creating the land. To aid them in this endeavor, the elder gods bestowed upon them a jeweled spear called the Ame-no-nuboko (Heavenly Jeweled Spear). Standing on the floating bridge of heaven, Izanagi and Izanami plunged the spear into the formless ocean below. As they lifted the spear from the water, droplets fell from its tip, solidifying into the first island, known as Onogoro-shima.

After descending to this newly formed island, Izanagi and Izanami decided to unite in marriage and create more land. They built a heavenly pillar, known as the Ame-no-mihashira, and circled it in opposite directions. Upon meeting on the other side, Izanami, in a display of eagerness, spoke first, greeting Izanagi. However, this breach of protocol led to the birth of malformed offspring, the Hiruko (Leech Child) and Awashima, who were abandoned. Recognizing that they had made a mistake, Izanagi and Izanami sought guidance from the elder gods, who informed them that Izanagi, as the male, should have spoken first during the ritual.

Following this divine instruction, Izanagi and Izanami performed the ritual again, this time correctly, and their union was blessed with success. From their union came the creation of the islands of Japan, known as the kuniumi (birth of the land). They gave birth to the eight large islands that constitute the Japanese archipelago: Awaji, Shikoku, Oki, Kyushu, Iki, Tsushima, Sado, and Honshu. These islands are collectively known as the Oyashima, or "eight great islands."

Following the creation of the land, Izanagi and Izanami continued to give birth to various kami, representing different elements of the natural world and human life. These included the kami of the seas, rivers, mountains, trees, and even the deities of food and agriculture. Through this process, the world became populated with divine beings, each governing specific aspects of existence.

However, the story of Izanagi and Izanami takes a tragic turn with the birth of Kagutsuchi, the god of fire. The birth of this fiery deity was so intense that it severely burned Izanami, leading to her death. Stricken with grief, Izanagi mourned the loss of his beloved wife, and from his tears and sorrow, more kami were born.

Izanagi, unable to accept Izanami's death, decided to journey to Yomi, the land of the dead, in an attempt to bring her back. Yomi is depicted as a dark and desolate place, a stark contrast to the vibrant and life-filled world that Izanagi and Izanami had created. Upon reaching Yomi, Izanagi found Izanami and pleaded with her to return to the land of the living. Izanami, however, informed him that she had already consumed the food of the underworld, binding her to Yomi. She agreed to consult with the gods of the underworld but asked Izanagi to wait for her and not to look upon her until she returned.

Overcome with impatience and curiosity, Izanagi broke his promise and lit a torch to see Izanami. To his horror, he found that she had transformed into a decaying, monstrous figure, surrounded by the maggots and spirits of the underworld. Disgusted and terrified, Izanagi fled, with the enraged Izanami pursuing him. As he escaped, Izanagi blocked the entrance to Yomi with a massive boulder, effectively separating the worlds of the living and the dead.

This event marked the final separation between Izanagi and Izanami. In her anger, Izanami vowed to kill one thousand people every day, to which Izanagi responded that he would ensure that fifteen hundred would be born each day, thus maintaining the balance of life and death. This exchange symbolizes the inevitable cycle of life and death that governs the natural world.

After his escape from Yomi, Izanagi felt the need to purify himself from the impurities of the underworld. This purification ritual, known as misogi, is a significant act in Shinto practice and is performed by Izanagi at a river. As he washed, new deities emerged from his body. Most notably, from his left eye came Amaterasu, the sun goddess; from his right eye, Tsukuyomi, the moon god; and from his nose, Susanoo, the storm god. These three deities would go on to play crucial roles in Japanese mythology, particularly in the narratives concerning the imperial family and the governance of the natural world.

The themes of creation, destruction, and purification are central to understanding the Shinto worldview, where the kami are deeply intertwined with the physical world. The narrative also emphasizes the importance of rituals, balance, and the cyclical nature of existence—concepts that remain integral to Japanese spirituality and culture.

The Birth of Amaterasu

Amaterasu's birth is closely connected to the myth of Izanagi and Izanami, the primordial deities who created the islands of Japan and gave birth to many of the gods. After the death of Izanami, Izanagi undertook a journey to the underworld, Yomi, in an attempt to retrieve his wife. However, his efforts failed, and he fled Yomi, horrified by the sight of Izanami's decayed form. Upon returning to the world of the living, Izanagi felt the need to purify himself from the defilement of the underworld. This purification ritual, known as misogi, took place in a river, and it was during this act that Amaterasu was born.

As Izanagi washed his face, three important deities emerged from the cleansing process. Amaterasu was born from his left eye, Tsukuyomi, the moon god, from his right eye, and Susanoo, the storm god, from his nose. The fact that Amaterasu emerged from Izanagi's left eye is symbolic, as the left side is traditionally associated with the heart and therefore with the central qualities of life and vitality. The brightness and warmth of the sun, embodied by Amaterasu, are thus seen as the life-giving forces that sustain the world.

Amaterasu's birth marked the beginning of a new cosmic order. As the goddess of the sun, she was given dominion over Takamagahara, the High Plain of Heaven, where the most powerful and significant deities resided. Her role as the sun goddess made her the source of light, warmth, and life, which are essential for the prosperity of the natural world and, by extension, human society. In Shinto belief, the sun is the most vital force in the universe, and Amaterasu, as its personification, holds unparalleled importance.

She is also seen as the divine ancestor of the Japanese imperial family. This connection is central to the mythological and historical narrative of Japan. According to the Kojiki and Nihon Shoki, Amaterasu sent her grandson, Ninigi-no-Mikoto, to earth to establish the imperial lineage. She entrusted him with the three sacred treasures—the mirror, the jewel, and the sword—that symbolized his divine authority. These treasures, known as the Imperial Regalia of Japan, are still integral to the enthronement ceremonies of Japanese emperors, symbolizing the continuity of the divine mandate that began with Amaterasu.

Amaterasu's story is also marked by a period of crisis that highlights her significance and the impact of her presence on the world. This crisis is best exemplified in the myth of the Amano-Iwato (Heavenly Rock Cave). According to the myth, Amaterasu's brother Susanoo, the storm god, caused great havoc in the heavens. His violent and disruptive behavior, which included destroying Amaterasu's rice fields, defiling her sacred weaving hall, and throwing a flayed horse into the hall, angered and deeply saddened her. In response, Amaterasu retreated into the Amano-Iwato, plunging the world into darkness.

Amaterasu's withdrawal had catastrophic consequences. Without the sun's light, crops withered, the land became cold and barren, and chaos spread across both the heavens and the earth. The other gods were alarmed by this and gathered to devise a plan to coax Amaterasu out of the cave. They tried various methods, including offering prayers and holding rituals, but nothing worked. Finally, the goddess Ame-no-Uzume performed a dance so outrageous and humorous that it made the other gods laugh uproariously. Curiosity piqued by the noise, Amaterasu peeked out of the cave, and at that moment, the god Ame-no-Koyane held up a mirror, reflecting Amaterasu's own radiant image back at her. Mesmerized by her reflection, Amaterasu was lured out of the cave, and light was restored to the world.

The significance of this myth is manifold. Her presence is vital for the continuation of life, and her withdrawal demonstrates the dire consequences of her absence. The episode also highlights the importance of rituals, festivals, and communal actions in Shinto practice. The collective effort of the gods to bring Amaterasu back symbolizes the power of unity and the communal nature of religious observance in Japanese culture.

Amaterasu's reemergence from the cave also symbolizes the triumph of order over chaos, light over darkness, and life over death. These themes are central to Shinto and are reflected in many aspects of Japanese culture, including its festivals, such as the annual Taisai at the Ise Grand Shrine, which is dedicated to Amaterasu. The Ise Shrine itself is the most important Shinto shrine in Japan, housing the mirror that represents Amaterasu and serving as the spiritual center of the nation.

The Descent of Ninigi

This myth, which is deeply embedded in the Shinto tradition, connects the ruling emperors of Japan directly to the gods, thereby establishing the concept of divine right and legitimizing their sovereignty. The story is found in the ancient texts of the Kojiki (Records of Ancient Matters) and Nihon Shoki (Chronicles of Japan), which are crucial sources for understanding Japan's mythological history and the religious underpinnings of the imperial institution.

The narrative begins with the reign of Amaterasu, the sun goddess and one of the most important deities in the Shinto pantheon. Amaterasu, who was born from the left eye of the primordial god Izanagi during his purification ritual, governs the heavens and is revered as the divine ancestor of the Japanese imperial family. Her grandson, Ninigi-no-Mikoto, is the central figure in this myth.

The myth unfolds against the backdrop of conflict in the heavenly realm. Amaterasu had originally sent her son, Ame-no-Oshihomimi, to rule over the earthly world. However, he returned to the heavens after witnessing the chaotic and unruly state of the land, which was populated by deities of a lesser order and unruly spirits. To restore order and establish a righteous rule on earth, Amaterasu convened a divine council of gods to decide who among them should descend to the earth and bring order.

After much deliberation, the council decided that Ninigi, Amaterasu's grandson, would be the one to descend. Amaterasu entrusted Ninigi with three sacred treasures—the Yata no Kagami (a mirror), the Yasakani no Magatama (a jewel), and the Kusanagi no Tsurugi (a sword). These treasures, collectively known as the Imperial Regalia of Japan, symbolize the legitimacy and divine authority of the emperor. The mirror represents wisdom and truth, the jewel embodies benevolence, and the sword signifies valor. Amaterasu's directive was clear: Ninigi was to descend to the earthly realm, pacify it, and establish a lineage that would rule Japan in accordance with divine will.

Ninigi's descent, accompanied by a retinue of gods, is a significant event in Japanese mythology. He descended from the heavens at a place called Takachiho, located in what is now Miyazaki Prefecture on the island of Kyushu. Takachiho is still revered as a sacred site, believed to be the very location where Ninigi set foot on earth. The place is marked by the Amano-Iwato Shrine, which is a testament to the enduring cultural and religious significance of this myth.

Upon his arrival, Ninigi encountered Sarutahiko, a powerful earth deity who initially resisted his descent. Sarutahiko was the leader of the earthly deities and held dominion over the land. However, after a brief confrontation, Sarutahiko recognized Ninigi's divine authority and offered his assistance in guiding the heavenly grandson to his destination. This encounter signifies the transition of power from the earthly spirits to the heavenly gods, marking the beginning of a new order under divine rule.

Ninigi's mission on earth was not merely to govern but to establish a dynasty that would carry on the divine mandate. He married Konohanasakuya-hime, a beautiful goddess associated with Mount Fuji and the sakura (cherry blossom). Their union produced three sons, who are considered the progenitors of the Japanese imperial family. The most prominent of these sons was Hoori, who would later become a central figure in another important myth involving the undersea palace of the dragon god Ryujin.

The significance of Ninigi's descent lies not only in the establishment of the imperial lineage but also in the concept of chokushin, or divine right, which asserts that the emperor is a direct descendant of the gods. This belief has been a cornerstone of the Japanese monarchy's legitimacy throughout history. It underpins the unique relationship between the emperor and the Shinto religion, where the emperor serves as both a political leader and a high priest, mediating between the gods and the people.

The myth also reflects the hierarchical structure of the Shinto pantheon, where certain gods are tasked with specific roles in maintaining cosmic order. Ninigi's descent represents the divine will to bring harmony and order to the world, a recurring theme in Shinto beliefs. The earthly realm, initially chaotic and dominated by lesser deities, becomes a place of order and civilization under the rule of the divine lineage established by Ninigi.

Over the centuries, the myth of Ninigi's descent has been invoked to justify the continuity and sanctity of the imperial line. During the Meiji Restoration in the 19th century, when Shinto was institutionalized as the state religion, the myth gained renewed significance. The restoration of the emperor's political power was seen as a return to the divine order established by Ninigi, further solidifying the emperor's role as a living god until the end of World War II. Even today, the symbols and rituals associated with the imperial family are deeply rooted in this myth. The three sacred treasures, although not publicly displayed, are integral to the enthronement ceremonies of Japanese emperors.

Susanoo: The Storm God

Susanoo is the brother of Amaterasu, the sun goddess, and Tsukuyomi, the moon god, all of whom were born from the purification ritual performed by their father, Izanagi. While Amaterasu is associated with light, order, and life, and Tsukuyomi with the calm and reflective qualities of the night, Susanoo is inherently connected with the chaotic and destructive forces of storms and the sea. His domain is the oceans and the storms that rage over them, symbolizing the fearsome power of nature that can bring both life-giving rain and devastating typhoons.

The complexity of Susanoo's character is first evident in his turbulent relationship with Amaterasu. Susanoo's behavior is often reckless and driven by intense emotions, which leads to conflict with his sister. One of the most famous myths involving Susanoo is his exile from the heavens after a series of destructive actions. After being commanded by their father, Izanagi, to leave Takamagahara (the High Plain of Heaven), Susanoo, instead of complying peacefully, chose to confront Amaterasu.

In this confrontation, Susanoo's actions escalated from mischievous to outright destructive. He destroyed Amaterasu's rice fields, defiled her sacred weaving hall by throwing a flayed horse into it, and generally caused chaos and disruption in the heavenly realm. These actions were not just rebellious but were symbolic of the storm god's ability to upend the natural and social order, reflecting the uncontrollable nature of storms and natural disasters. Amaterasu, deeply distressed by Susanoo's actions, retreated into the Amano-Iwato (Heavenly Rock Cave), plunging the world into darkness. This event, which threatened the balance of the cosmos, highlighted the destructive potential of Susanoo's nature.

However, Susanoo's character is not defined solely by his destructive tendencies. He is also capable of acts of great heroism and benevolence. This dual nature is perhaps best exemplified in the myth of his battle with the monstrous serpent, Yamata no Orochi. After being exiled from the heavens for his transgressions, Susanoo descended to the earth, where he encountered an elderly couple weeping over their last remaining daughter. The couple, who were the earthly deities Ashinazuchi and Tenazuchi, told Susanoo that they had lost seven of their eight daughters to the fearsome Yamata no Orochi, a gigantic serpent with eight heads and eight tails. The monster was demanding their final daughter, Kushinadahime, as its next victim.

Moved by their plight, Susanoo devised a plan to defeat the serpent. He transformed Kushinadahime into a comb and placed her in his hair for safekeeping. He then instructed the couple to prepare eight vats of sake (rice wine) and place them around their home. When Yamata no Orochi arrived, it drank the sake from the vats, becoming intoxicated. As the serpent lay in a stupor, Susanoo attacked it, cutting off its heads and tails. In the tail of the serpent, Susanoo discovered the legendary sword, Kusanagi-no-Tsurugi (Grass-Cutting Sword), which he later presented to Amaterasu as a gesture of reconciliation. This sword would become one of the three sacred treasures of the Japanese imperial regalia.

This episode demonstrates Susanoo's capacity for heroism and his protective instincts. His actions saved Kushinadahime and vanquished a great evil, showing that despite his earlier destructive behavior, Susanoo could also be a force for good. The myth of Yamata no Orochi emphasizes the duality of Susanoo's character: while he is capable of great destruction, he also possesses the strength and bravery to combat evil and protect the vulnerable.

In many myths, he oscillates between being a disruptor and a benefactor. For example, after his battle with Yamata no

Orochi, Susanoo married Kushinadahime and established a family, becoming a deity associated with the protection of rice fields and agriculture—a far cry from his earlier role as a destroyer of crops. This transformation highlights the idea that even the most chaotic and destructive forces can be harnessed for positive purposes when properly directed.

In Shinto, nature is seen as inherently balanced, with all aspects—whether destructive or nurturing—being necessary for the harmony of the world. Susanoo, as a deity who embodies both extremes, represents this balance. His actions remind us that the forces of nature, while often unpredictable and fearsome, are also essential for life and renewal.

Moreover, Susanoo's narrative arc—from a god of chaos and destruction to a hero and protector—also serves as a powerful symbol of redemption and transformation. His ability to evolve and change reflects the Shinto belief in the possibility of purification and renewal, both for individuals and the world itself.

Tsukuyomi: The Moon God

The origins of Tsukuyomi are rooted in the creation myths of Japan. He, along with Amaterasu and Susanoo, was born from the purification ritual of Izanagi, the primordial god who, after escaping from the underworld, Yomi, sought to cleanse himself of the impurities of death. During this ritual, Izanagi washed his right eye, from which Tsukuyomi emerged, symbolizing the birth of the moon. This association with the right eye, traditionally considered a place of reflection and intuition, aligns with the moon's connection to the night and its contemplative, mysterious qualities.

Tsukuyomi's realm is the night sky, where he governs over the moon and the passage of time as it waxes and wanes. In contrast to his sister Amaterasu, who embodies the brilliance and vitality of the sun, Tsukuyomi is often depicted as a calm, stoic figure, reflecting the quiet and serene nature of the moon. The moon's cycle, with its phases of growth and decline, is seen as a symbol of renewal and the passage of time, echoing the Shinto belief in the cyclical nature of life and the universe.

Despite his significant role, Tsukuyomi's presence in Japanese mythology is somewhat enigmatic, with fewer myths and stories dedicated to him compared to Amaterasu and Susanoo. This relative obscurity may be partly due to his character and the events that led to his estrangement from Amaterasu, which resulted in a symbolic separation of the sun and the moon in Japanese cosmology.

One of the most notable myths involving Tsukuyomi is the story of how he came to be separated from his sister Amaterasu. According to the *Nihon Shoki* (Chronicles of Japan), Tsukuyomi was sent by Amaterasu as her representative to attend a feast hosted by Uke Mochi, the goddess of food. During the feast, Uke Mochi produced food by expelling it from her mouth, nose, and other orifices, an act that disgusted Tsukuyomi. Offended by what he perceived as a vile and disrespectful act, Tsukuyomi killed Uke Mochi in a fit of rage.

When Amaterasu learned of Tsukuyomi's actions, she was horrified by his violence. She declared that she could no longer bear to look upon her brother and banished him from her presence. This decree symbolically explains why the sun and the moon are never seen together in the sky, marking the separation of day and night. Tsukuyomi's act and subsequent banishment emphasize the themes of purity, order, and the consequences of violating sacred customs, which are central to Shinto beliefs.

Tsukuyomi's estrangement from Amaterasu also represents the inherent tension between light and darkness, a duality that is essential to the balance of the world. In Shinto, this duality is not seen as a conflict but as a necessary balance that sustains the natural order. The separation of the sun and the moon ensures that both day and night have their rightful place, each playing a crucial role in the cycle of life.

Despite this myth, which casts Tsukuyomi in a negative light, he is not regarded as an evil deity. Instead, he embodies the more austere and mysterious aspects of nature. The moon, after all, is a source of light in the darkness, guiding travelers at night and influencing the tides, a vital force for life on earth. Tsukuyomi's role as the moon god also connects him to timekeeping and calendars, as the phases of the moon have historically been used to measure time in many cultures, including Japan. The lunar calendar, which was once widely used in Japan, reflects Tsukuyomi's influence on the cycles of months and seasons, marking the passage of time in harmony with nature.

Tsukuyomi's worship, like that of many Shinto deities, is closely tied to natural phenomena. Shrines dedicated to him are less common than those for Amaterasu, but he is still honored in various rituals and festivals that celebrate the moon. One such event is the *Tsukimi* (moon viewing) festival, which takes place in the autumn when the moon is believed to be at its brightest and most beautiful. During this festival, offerings of rice dumplings, seasonal fruits, and sake are made to the moon in appreciation of its beauty and its role in the natural cycles of the year.

In addition to his association with the moon and time, Tsukuyomi is also sometimes linked to other aspects of Japanese culture and spirituality. For instance, the concept of *yohaku*, or the beauty of empty space and quiet contemplation, can be related to Tsukuyomi's serene and reflective nature. The moon, often depicted in Japanese art and poetry as a solitary figure in the night sky, inspires a sense of peace and introspection, qualities that are central to Tsukuyomi's character.

Inari: the God of Rice

The origins of Inari are somewhat enigmatic, with different traditions and interpretations contributing to a multifaceted identity. Inari is often depicted as a genderless or androgynous deity, but can also be portrayed as male, female, or a collective of deities. This flexibility in gender and form reflects the universal and adaptable nature of Inari, allowing for the deity's worship to be integrated into various local customs and practices. The most common form of Inari worship, however, centers around the deity's association with rice, a staple of the Japanese diet and a symbol of life and prosperity.

Rice cultivation has been a cornerstone of Japanese society for millennia, and Inari, as the god of rice, became intrinsically linked to the well-being of the nation. The connection between Inari and rice goes beyond mere agricultural importance; it represents a deeper spiritual connection to the cycles of nature and the divine forces that ensure the fertility of the land. As a result, Inari is often invoked for blessings of good harvests, protection of crops, and general prosperity.

One of the most distinctive features of Inari's worship is the presence of foxes, known as *kitsune*, which are considered the deity's messengers. The relationship between Inari and foxes is complex and rich with symbolism. Kitsune are often depicted as intelligent, shape-shifting creatures with the ability to transform into human form. Inari's foxes are believed to possess both benevolent and mischievous qualities, embodying the duality of nature itself. They are revered for their role in protecting the rice fields and bringing prosperity, but they are also feared for their potential to cause mischief if not properly respected.

The foxes of Inari are commonly portrayed in statues found at Inari shrines, often with one holding a key in its mouth, symbolizing the protection of the rice granaries. These statues are typically placed at the entrance of shrines, creating a protective barrier between the sacred space and the outside world. The foxes' association with Inari has also led to the belief that they can serve as intermediaries between humans and the deity, carrying prayers and messages to the divine.

The most famous and significant shrine dedicated to Inari is Fushimi Inari Taisha, located in Kyoto. Fushimi Inari is the head shrine among thousands of Inari shrines spread across Japan, and it is one of the oldest and most important religious sites in the country. Established in 711 CE, Fushimi Inari Taisha is renowned for its thousands of vermilion *torii* gates, which create a striking pathway up the sacred Mount Inari. These gates, donated by individuals and businesses, reflect the deep veneration of Inari as a bringer of prosperity and success.

The worship at Fushimi Inari Taisha and other Inari shrines involves rituals and offerings that are deeply tied to agricultural cycles. Offerings of rice, sake, and other foodstuffs are made to ensure the favor of Inari, particularly during key agricultural events such as planting and harvest seasons. In addition to agricultural offerings, small *kitsune* figurines, coins, and other symbols of wealth and protection are also common offerings.

Inari's association with prosperity has also led to a strong connection with the arts, particularly in the realms of theater and literature. Inari is frequently invoked by actors, writers, and other artists seeking inspiration and success in their creative endeavors. This relationship between Inari and the arts is a testament to the deity's expansive influence and the way in which Inari has been embraced by various segments of society.

In addition to the Shinto tradition, Inari has been syncretized with Buddhist practices, further broadening the scope of worship. In the context of Buddhism, Inari is often identified with the goddess Dakiniten, who shares similar attributes of fertility, prosperity, and protection. This syncretism illustrates the fluidity of religious practices in Japan, where deities from different traditions can merge and coexist within a single religious framework.

Despite the widespread reverence for Inari, the deity's character remains somewhat elusive and enigmatic. This ambiguity allows for a wide range of interpretations and practices associated with Inari, making the deity accessible to people from all walks of life. Whether as a god of rice, a patron of commerce, or a protector of the arts, Inari's role in Japanese culture is both expansive and deeply ingrained.

Inari's significance is further highlighted by the annual festivals held in the deity's honor. The most notable of these is the Fushimi Inari Taisha's New Year's festival, where thousands of worshippers visit the shrine to pray for a prosperous year ahead. These festivals, which often involve processions, performances, and the offering of rice and sake, serve to renew the community's connection with Inari and reinforce the deity's central role in ensuring the well-being of the people.

Hachiman: The God of War

Known as the god of war, archery, and the protector of Japan, Hachiman is also deeply associated with the imperial family and is often regarded as the divine protector of the Japanese nation. Over time, Hachiman's worship has evolved, reflecting the changing social, political, and religious landscapes of Japan.

The origins of Hachiman are somewhat unique compared to other deities in the Japanese pantheon. Unlike many Shinto kami who are tied to natural elements or ancestral spirits, Hachiman is believed to have originated as a deified historical figure. According to legend, Hachiman is the deification of Emperor Ōjin, the fifteenth emperor of Japan, who reigned in the late 3rd and early 4th centuries. After his death, Emperor Ōjin was worshipped as a god, and over time, his cult grew, blending with pre-existing local deities and beliefs, eventually becoming the syncretic figure known as Hachiman.

Hachiman's association with war and martial prowess is one of his most defining characteristics. During the Heian period (794-1185), as the samurai class rose to prominence, Hachiman became increasingly venerated as the god of warriors. Samurai worshipped Hachiman for protection in battle, guidance in military strategy, and success in their martial endeavors. This veneration was not only a personal or local practice but also institutionalized within the military and political spheres of Japan. Hachiman's status as the protector of warriors made him an essential figure in the religious practices of the samurai, who saw themselves as carrying out the divine will in their pursuit of honor and duty.

The symbolism of archery, which is closely associated with Hachiman, also highlights his connection to the warrior class. Archery was a highly respected martial skill in Japan, symbolizing both the physical and spiritual discipline required of a warrior. Hachiman, as the god of war and archery, was invoked to bless the arrows and bows of the samurai, ensuring their accuracy and effectiveness in battle. This relationship between Hachiman and archery further solidified his role as the protector and guide of the warrior class.

In addition to his role as the god of war, Hachiman is also revered as a protector of Japan and its people. This protective aspect of Hachiman is particularly evident in his association with the imperial family and the broader concept of national defense. Hachiman's connection to the imperial family is most clearly seen in the historical narratives that link him to the legendary Empress Jingu, who is said to have led a successful military campaign in Korea with the divine assistance of Hachiman. According to the legend, after her victory, Empress Jingū became pregnant with Emperor Ōjin, who was later deified as Hachiman. This story not only reinforces Hachiman's martial prowess but also establishes his divine connection to the imperial lineage, further legitimizing the emperor's divine right to rule.

Hachiman's role as the protector of Japan was particularly emphasized during periods of foreign threat. One of the most famous examples is during the Mongol invasions of Japan in the 13th century. The Japanese attributed their miraculous survival to the divine intervention of Hachiman, who was believed to have sent the *kamikaze* (divine wind) that destroyed the invading Mongol fleets. This event solidified Hachiman's reputation as the guardian of the Japanese nation, a role that continued to be invoked in subsequent centuries whenever Japan faced external threats.

The spread of Hachiman worship throughout Japan is evident in the vast number of shrines dedicated to him. There are over 30,000 Hachiman shrines across Japan, making him one of the most widely venerated deities in the country. The most important of these is the Usa Jingū in Oita Prefecture, which is considered the head shrine of Hachiman worship. Usa Jingū is believed to be the original site where Hachiman was first enshrined, and it has played a central role in the religious and political history of Japan. Pilgrimages to Usa Jingū and other Hachiman shrines have been common throughout Japanese history, particularly among warriors seeking the god's protection and favor.

Hachiman's worship is also deeply intertwined with the cultural and spiritual practices of Japan. Festivals dedicated to Hachiman, such as the *Hōjō-e* (Rite of Release of Living Beings), which originated at the Usa Jingū, reflect the deity's role in promoting peace and the sanctity of life. These festivals often involve rituals that emphasize purification, offerings of food and sake, and the release of captive animals, symbolizing the restoration of balance and harmony in the world.

Despite his origins as a god of war, Hachiman's role in Japanese mythology and religion is far from one-dimensional. He is a protector of the nation, a guardian of the imperial family, a patron of the warrior class, and a deity who ensures the fertility and prosperity of the land. This multifaceted nature of Hachiman reflects the complexity of Japanese religious beliefs, where deities often serve multiple roles and are worshipped in various contexts depending on the needs of the people and the times.

Chapter Two: Heroes and Legendary Figures

Jimmu: The first Emperor of Japan

Emperor Jimmu's journey to unify Japan is not only a tale of conquest and state-building but also one that establishes the divine origins of the Japanese imperial line, a theme that has profoundly influenced Japan's cultural and political identity.

According to legend, Jimmu was born as Kamuyamato Iwarebiko, a descendant of the sun goddess Amaterasu. His lineage is traced back to Ninigi-no-Mikoto, Amaterasu's grandson, who was sent to earth to rule over Japan. This divine ancestry is crucial in establishing the legitimacy of the imperial family, asserting that the emperors of Japan are direct descendants of the gods, with a divine mandate to rule the land.

The story of Jimmu's rise to power begins in the region of Kyushu, in southern Japan, where he and his brothers were born and raised. As he matured, Jimmu demonstrated remarkable leadership qualities and an unyielding resolve to expand his influence beyond Kyushu. At that time, Japan was a fragmented land, inhabited by various tribes and clans, each with its own territory and leadership. Jimmu's ambition was to unify these disparate groups under his rule, establishing a central authority that would bring order and stability to the land.

Jimmu's journey toward unification began when he and his brothers set out from Kyushu to the eastern regions of Japan, an area that was believed to be more favorable for establishing a new seat of power. Their journey was not without challenges, as they encountered resistance from local chieftains and faced the harsh realities of travel in ancient Japan. The route they took led them through rugged terrain and required them to cross the treacherous Seto Inland Sea.

One of the key moments in Jimmu's journey occurred when the expedition encountered a powerful chieftain named Nagasunehiko, who ruled over the land of Yamato. Nagasunehiko fiercely resisted Jimmu's advance, leading to a significant battle that would determine the fate of Jimmu's campaign. According to the myth, Jimmu's forces initially struggled against Nagasunehiko's superior knowledge of the terrain and his powerful army. However, it was at this moment that the divine intervention of the gods played a crucial role in Jimmu's victory.

Recognizing the strategic disadvantage posed by facing the enemy while advancing eastward into the rising sun, Jimmu and his forces were said to be blinded by the sun's glare, a sign that the gods were displeased. Jimmu, understanding the spiritual significance of this omen, retreated and regrouped, praying to Amaterasu for guidance and support. In response to his prayers, Amaterasu sent a sacred bird known as the *Yatagarasu*, a three-legged crow, to guide Jimmu's forces. The appearance of Yatagarasu was seen as a divine sign, providing Jimmu with the confidence and strategic advantage he needed to ultimately defeat Nagasunehiko and secure control over Yamato.

With the defeat of Nagasunehiko and the conquest of Yamato, Jimmu established his capital at Kashihara, in present-day Nara Prefecture. This marked the beginning of a unified Japan under a central authority, with Jimmu as its first emperor. His accession to the throne in 660 BCE is traditionally celebrated as the founding of the Japanese nation, a date that has been commemorated throughout history and is still observed today as National Foundation Day (Kenkoku Kinen no Hi) on February 11.

Jimmu's establishment of the Yamato state is a foundational myth that has shaped the identity and continuity of the Japanese imperial institution. The narrative of divine descent and the role of the gods in legitimizing his rule provided a powerful ideological framework that reinforced the emperor's role as both a political and spiritual leader. This divine mandate not only justified the authority of Jimmu and his descendants but also established the emperor as a living deity, an embodiment of the divine will on earth.

The story of Emperor Jimmu also highlights the values that were central to the early Japanese state. His journey to unify Japan reflects ideals of bravery, perseverance, and piety. Jimmu's reliance on divine guidance and his willingness to heed the omens and signs from the gods underscored the importance of maintaining harmony with the divine order, a concept that would continue to influence Japanese governance and religious practices for centuries.

The legacy of Emperor Jimmu extends far beyond the mythological narrative. Throughout Japanese history, successive emperors and political leaders have invoked Jimmu's legacy to legitimize their own authority and to promote a sense of national unity. During the Meiji Restoration in the late 19th century, when Japan underwent a period of rapid modernization and the restoration of imperial power, the figure of Jimmu was prominently featured as a symbol of Japan's ancient origins and its continuity as a unified state. The Meiji government used Jimmu's myth to foster a sense of patriotism and to solidify the emperor's role as the central figure of the nation.

In modern Japan, Emperor Jimmu remains an important cultural and historical figure. His story is taught in schools, celebrated in festivals, and remembered in various forms of art and literature. The Kashihara Shrine, built near the site of his legendary capital, serves as a place of worship and a symbol of his enduring legacy. The shrine, along with other sites associated with Jimmu, attracts visitors who seek to connect with the origins of the Japanese nation and to honor the first emperor who, according to tradition, laid the foundations for the country as it exists today.

Yamato Takeru

As a warrior of unparalleled skill and bravery, Prince Yamato Takeru's exploits across Japan are emblematic of the heroic ideal in Japanese culture, and his story has left a lasting impact on the nation's historical and cultural identity.

Yamato Takeru was born as Prince Ōsu, the son of Emperor Keikō, who reigned during the late first century AD. From an early age, Prince Ōsu demonstrated exceptional martial abilities, but also a fierce and ruthless nature. One of the earliest tales of his exploits involves the killing of his older brother, Prince Ōusu, whom he viewed as a rival. This act of fratricide, though heinous, highlighted his determination and set the stage for his later exploits. As punishment for his brother's murder, Emperor Keikō sent Ōsu on a series of dangerous missions, which were intended to either test his abilities or, perhaps, lead to his demise.

The first of these missions was against the Kumaso, a rebellious tribe in the southern regions of Kyushu. Disguising himself as a maidservant to infiltrate the enemy's stronghold, Ōsu managed to get close to the leaders of the Kumaso during a banquet. At the opportune moment, he revealed his identity and struck down the Kumaso chieftains with his sword. It was during this encounter that one of the dying chieftains, impressed by the young prince's bravery and skill, gave him the name Yamato Takeru, meaning "the Brave of Yamato." This name, combining the ancient province of Yamato with the epithet of bravery, solidified his identity as a hero of the Yamato state, the precursor to the unified Japanese nation.

Following his success against the Kumaso, Yamato Takeru was sent on another mission to subdue the Emishi, a people who lived in the northeastern region of Japan. This campaign took him to the eastern provinces, where he continued to demonstrate his strategic prowess and martial strength. However, it was on this journey that he faced some of his most formidable challenges, which would eventually lead to his tragic downfall.

One of the most famous episodes in Yamato Takeru's story is his encounter with the fire god and the subsequent acquisition of the legendary sword Kusanagi-no-Tsurugi (Grass-Cutting Sword), which was a gift from his aunt, the sun goddess Amaterasu, who had originally entrusted the sword to the imperial family. The sword, along with other sacred treasures, symbolized divine authority and protection. According to the legend, Yamato Takeru was ambushed in a field of tall grass by an enemy who set the grass ablaze in an attempt to kill him. Using Kusanagi-no-Tsurugi, Yamato Takeru not only cut down the grass to prevent the fire from reaching him but also created a backfire that turned the flames against his enemies, securing his victory. This episode highlights Yamato Takeru's resourcefulness and the divine favor he enjoyed, as the sword became a symbol of his heroic status.

However, despite his many victories, Yamato Takeru’s life was marked by an undercurrent of tragedy. After his campaign in the east, he was sent on another mission to the Ise Province, where he sought the blessing of the great sun goddess Amaterasu at her shrine. There, he was warned by the priests that his journey would be perilous and that he should not underestimate the dangers he faced. Despite this warning, Yamato Takeru pressed on, confident in his strength and the divine protection he believed he carried.

Tragically, Yamato Takeru's confidence led to his undoing. On his return journey, he encountered the god of Mount Ibuki, whom he did not recognize as a deity. Disregarding the god's power, Yamato Takeru continued on his way, only to be struck down by a sudden illness, which was a divine retribution for his arrogance. Stricken with this mysterious illness, he wandered the wilderness, gradually losing his strength. His final moments were spent in a remote field, where, in his last breath, he lamented his fate, cursing the eastern lands for their treachery. According to legend, his spirit transformed into a great white bird, which flew away, symbolizing his transcendence from the mortal world.

Yamato Takeru's death was deeply mourned, and his legacy became enshrined in Japanese culture as the archetype of the tragic hero—one who, despite immense strength and valor, ultimately succumbs to fate. The places associated with his life and death, such as Mount Ibuki and the plain where he died, became sites of pilgrimage and worship. Shrines dedicated to Yamato Takeru, such as the Omiwa Shrine in Nara and the Taga Shrine in Shiga, honor his memory and continue to attract devotees who seek his protection and blessings.

Yamato Takeru's story, while deeply rooted in myth, reflects the historical realities of early Japan, where the unification of the country and the subjugation of various regional tribes were critical to the formation of the Japanese state. His exploits across Japan symbolize the expansion of the Yamato state's influence and the centralization of power under the imperial family. Moreover, his tale embodies the values of bravery, loyalty, and sacrifice, which have been central to Japanese warrior culture throughout history.

In addition to his historical and cultural significance, Yamato Takeru's story has also inspired numerous works of literature, theater, and art. His character has been depicted in *Noh* plays, *Kabuki* theater, and modern media, where he continues to be a symbol of Japan's heroic past. His life and deeds are celebrated as part of the broader narrative of Japan's divine origins and the enduring strength of the Japanese people.

Momotaro: The Peach Boy

The adventures of Momotaro against the oni, or demons, are deeply embedded in Japanese folklore, making him a cultural icon whose story reflects the values and ideals of Japanese society.

The tale of Momotaro begins with his miraculous birth. According to the most popular version of the legend, an elderly couple living in the countryside found a giant peach floating down a river. When they retrieved the peach and cut it open, they were astonished to find a healthy baby boy inside. Overjoyed by this miraculous event, the couple, who had long been childless, decided to raise the boy as their own and named him Momotaro, which translates to "Peach Boy." The name "Momo" means peach, and "Taro" is a common name for the eldest son in Japan.

From the beginning, it was clear that Momotaro was no ordinary child. He grew up to be strong, brave, and kind-hearted, embodying the qualities of an ideal hero. As Momotaro matured, he learned about the plight of his village, which was being terrorized by oni who lived on a distant island. These demons would regularly raid the village, stealing food, valuables, and sometimes even people. The villagers lived in fear of these oni, who were said to be monstrous beings with incredible strength and a fierce appetite for destruction.

Determined to protect his family and village, Momotaro decided to confront the oni and put an end to their terror. With the blessings of his adoptive parents, who provided him with provisions of *kibi dango* (millet dumplings), Momotaro set off on his journey. The millet dumplings, a symbol of sustenance and strength, would play a crucial role in the adventures that followed.

As Momotaro journeyed toward the oni's island, he encountered several animals along the way: a dog, a monkey, and a pheasant. Each of these animals initially posed a challenge to Momotaro, but he cleverly won them over by offering them his millet dumplings. In return for his generosity, the animals pledged their loyalty to Momotaro and joined him on his quest to defeat the oni. This alliance between Momotaro and the animals is a significant aspect of the story, emphasizing the themes of cooperation, loyalty, and the importance of forming alliances to achieve a common goal.

With his newfound companions, Momotaro finally reached the island where the oni resided. The island, often depicted as a dark and foreboding place, was heavily fortified and populated by fearsome demons. Undeterred by the daunting task ahead, Momotaro and his animal friends launched their assault on the oni's stronghold. The dog, with its keen sense of smell and fierce loyalty, helped locate the oni and guard against surprise attacks. The monkey, agile and quick, was able to scale the walls and disrupt the oni's defenses. The pheasant, with its ability to fly, provided aerial reconnaissance and could strike from above, adding an element of surprise to their attack.

The battle between Momotaro's small but determined group and the powerful oni is the climax of the story. Despite the overwhelming odds, Momotaro's bravery and the cooperation of his animal companions enabled them to overcome the demons. The oni, though strong and fearsome, were ultimately no match for Momotaro's courage and the strategic teamwork of the group. In some versions of the tale, Momotaro is depicted using his wits and the strength of his magical sword to defeat the oni's leader, while in others, it is the combined effort of the entire group that leads to victory.

After the battle, the defeated oni, recognizing Momotaro's strength and virtue, pleaded for mercy. In a display of his noble character, Momotaro spared their lives on the condition that they would never again terrorize his village or any other. The oni agreed, and as a gesture of goodwill, they offered up their stolen treasures, which Momotaro took back to his village.

Momotaro's return to his village was a moment of great celebration. He was hailed as a hero who had not only defeated the oni but also restored peace and prosperity to the land. The treasure he brought back helped to enrich the lives of the villagers, and his story became a source of inspiration for future generations.

As a hero, Momotaro represents the ideal virtues of courage, kindness, and filial piety. His willingness to risk his life to protect his village reflects the strong sense of duty and loyalty that is highly valued in Japanese culture. The use of millet dumplings to win over his animal companions symbolizes the power of generosity and cooperation, suggesting that even the most daunting challenges can be overcome through unity and mutual support.

Moreover, the story of Momotaro can be seen as an allegory for the broader struggles between good and evil, civilization and barbarism. The oni, with their monstrous appearance and destructive behavior, represent the chaotic forces that threaten the harmony of society. Momotaro, in contrast, embodies the civilizing force that restores order and peace. His victory over the oni is not just a physical triumph but also a moral one, reinforcing the idea that righteousness and virtue will ultimately prevail.

Kintaro: The Golden Boy

The story of Kintaro is one of resilience and transformation, as he rises from a life in the wilderness to become a legendary warrior. According to legend, Kintaro was born with the name Kaidomaru. His mother, Yaegiri, was of noble birth, but his early life was marked by hardship. In many versions of the story, his father was a high-ranking samurai, and his mother was forced to flee with her infant son after his father was killed or disgraced in some way. To protect her child from the dangers of the world, Yaegiri took refuge in the mountains, where she lived in isolation, raising Kintaro in the wilds of Mount Ashigara.

It is within these rugged, natural surroundings that Kintaro's character was forged. From a young age, Kintaro exhibited extraordinary physical strength and an innate connection with the natural world. He was often depicted as a robust child with bright red skin, carrying a large axe and wearing a simple loincloth. Kintaro's unusual appearance and prodigious strength set him apart from ordinary children, and he quickly became known as the "Golden Boy" due to his seemingly superhuman abilities and his warm, golden-hearted nature.

Kintaro's upbringing in the mountains was unconventional, to say the least. His mother, recognizing his special qualities, allowed him to roam freely in the wilderness, where he befriended the animals of the forest. In many stories, Kintaro is depicted as a friend to all creatures, capable of communicating with animals and understanding their ways. He was known to wrestle with bears, play with monkeys, and even ride on the backs of deer. These animals, in turn, respected Kintaro and followed him loyally, acknowledging him as a leader of the forest.

One of the most fascinating aspects of Kintaro's story is his relationship with a mountain witch, known as Yamauba or Yamanba, depending on the version of the tale. Yamauba, often portrayed as a supernatural being or a kindly but powerful old woman, played a crucial role in Kintaro's upbringing. Despite her fearsome reputation, Yamauba is depicted in this context as a maternal figure who takes Kintaro under her wing, teaching him the ways of the mountains and the secrets of nature. Under her guidance, Kintaro's strength and abilities grew, preparing him for the challenges that lay ahead.

As Kintaro matured, his reputation as a formidable and kind-hearted boy spread beyond the confines of the forest. His adventures and acts of bravery became known to humans who lived near the mountains, and stories of the Golden Boy's deeds were told far and wide. One of the most famous tales involves Kintaro single-handedly capturing a notorious robber who had been terrorizing the local villages. In this story, Kintaro's incredible strength and quick thinking allowed him to outwit and overpower the criminal, bringing peace to the troubled region.

Kintaro's journey from a wild child of the mountains to a respected warrior culminated when he was discovered by Minamoto no Yorimitsu, a legendary samurai and demon-slayer. Yorimitsu, also known as Raiko, was a warrior of great renown, and he immediately recognized Kintaro's potential. Impressed by the boy's strength, courage, and moral integrity, Yorimitsu offered to take Kintaro under his tutelage and train him as a samurai.

This moment marked a significant turning point in Kintaro's life. Leaving the mountains and his animal friends behind, Kintaro accepted the offer and took on a new name, Sakata no Kintoki, as a symbol of his new identity as a warrior. Under Yorimitsu's guidance, Kintaro honed his skills in martial arts, strategy, and swordsmanship, quickly becoming one of the most formidable warriors of his time. He served loyally alongside Yorimitsu and his band of legendary warriors, known as the Four Heavenly Kings, who were renowned for their bravery and strength in battling supernatural threats and protecting the land.

Kintaro's most famous exploit during this period was his role in the defeat of the Shuten-doji, a fearsome oni (demon) that terrorized the region of Mount Oe. According to the legend, Shuten-doji was a powerful and malevolent demon who kidnapped young women and held them captive in his mountain fortress. Yorimitsu, with the help of Kintaro and the other Heavenly Kings, devised a plan to infiltrate the fortress and defeat the demon. Disguised as mountain priests, they gained entry to Shuten-doji's lair, where they managed to intoxicate the demon with poisoned sake. In a fierce battle, Kintaro and his comrades ultimately defeated Shuten-doji, rescuing the captives and bringing an end to the demon's reign of terror.

This victory solidified Kintaro's reputation as a legendary warrior, and he became a celebrated figure in Japanese folklore. His journey from a child raised in the wilderness by a mountain witch to a heroic samurai embodies the ideals of perseverance, loyalty, and the triumph of good over evil. Kintaro's story is not only a tale of physical strength but also one of moral character, as he consistently used his abilities to protect the weak and uphold justice.

In Japanese culture, Kintaro has become a symbol of strength, resilience, and good fortune. His image is often depicted in art, literature, and popular media, where he is portrayed as a robust, red-skinned boy wielding an axe, surrounded by his animal companions. During the annual Boys' Day (now part of Children's Day, celebrated on May

5th), koinobori (carp-shaped streamers) and Kintaro dolls are displayed to inspire children with the virtues of courage, strength, and determination.

Minamoto no Yorimitsu (Raikō)

Raikō was born in 948 AD during the Heian period, a time characterized by the growing influence of the warrior class and the increasing instability in Japan. He was a scion of the prestigious Minamoto clan, which was one of the four great families that dominated Japanese politics and military affairs during this era. The Minamoto clan, also known as the Genji, would later play a crucial role in the establishment of the first shogunate, and Raikō's exploits contributed significantly to the clan's enduring legacy.

From a young age, Raikō displayed exceptional martial prowess and intelligence, quickly rising through the ranks to become one of the most trusted generals of the imperial court. His early career was marked by his involvement in suppressing various rebellions and protecting the capital, Kyoto, from external threats. However, it is his legendary encounters with supernatural beings that have made Raikō a household name in Japanese mythology.

Determined to protect his family and village, Momotaro decided to confront the oni and put an end to their terror. With the blessings of his adoptive parents, who provided him with provisions of *kibi dango* (millet dumplings), Momotaro set off on his journey. The millet dumplings, a symbol of sustenance and strength, would play a crucial role in the adventures that followed.

As Momotaro journeyed toward the oni's island, he encountered several animals along the way: a dog, a monkey, and a pheasant. Each of these animals initially posed a challenge to Momotaro, but he cleverly won them over by offering them his millet dumplings. In return for his generosity, the animals pledged their loyalty to Momotaro and joined him on his quest to defeat the oni. This alliance between Momotaro and the animals is a significant aspect of the story, emphasizing the themes of cooperation, loyalty, and the importance of forming alliances to achieve a common goal.

With his newfound companions, Momotaro finally reached the island where the oni resided. The island, often depicted as a dark and foreboding place, was heavily fortified and populated by fearsome demons. Undeterred by the daunting task ahead, Momotaro and his animal friends launched their assault on the oni's stronghold. The dog, with its keen sense of smell and fierce loyalty, helped locate the oni and guard against surprise attacks. The monkey, agile and quick, was able to scale the walls and disrupt the oni's defenses. The pheasant, with its ability to fly, provided aerial reconnaissance and could strike from above, adding an element of surprise to their attack.

The battle between Momotaro's small but determined group and the powerful oni is the climax of the story. Despite the overwhelming odds, Momotaro's bravery and the cooperation of his animal companions enabled them to overcome the demons. The oni, though strong and fearsome, were ultimately no match for Momotaro's courage and the strategic teamwork of the group. In some versions of the tale, Momotaro is depicted using his wits and the strength of his magical sword to defeat the oni's leader, while in others, it is the combined effort of the entire group that leads to victory.

After the battle, the defeated oni, recognizing Momotaro's strength and virtue, pleaded for mercy. In a display of his noble character, Momotaro spared their lives on the condition that they would never again terrorize his village or any other. The oni agreed, and as a gesture of goodwill, they offered up their stolen treasures, which Momotaro took back to his village.

Momotaro's return to his village was a moment of great celebration. He was hailed as a hero who had not only defeated the oni but also restored peace and prosperity to the land. The treasure he brought back helped to enrich the lives of the villagers, and his story became a source of inspiration for future generations.

The tale of Momotaro is rich with symbolic meaning and cultural significance. As a hero, Momotaro represents the ideal virtues of courage, kindness, and filial piety. His willingness to risk his life to protect his village reflects the strong sense of duty and loyalty that is highly valued in Japanese culture. The use of millet dumplings to win over his animal companions symbolizes the power of generosity and cooperation, suggesting that even the most daunting challenges can be overcome through unity and mutual support.

Moreover, the story of Momotaro can be seen as an allegory for the broader struggles between good and evil, civilization and barbarism. The oni, with their monstrous appearance and destructive behavior, represent the chaotic forces that threaten the harmony of society. Momotaro, in contrast, embodies the civilizing force that restores order and peace. His victory over the oni is not just a physical triumph but also a moral one, reinforcing the idea that righteousness and virtue will ultimately prevail.

Tawara Tōda – The Rice Bale Warrior

Tawara Tōda, whose real name was Fujiwara no Hidesato, was a nobleman and warrior during the Heian period (794–1185). He is best known for his legendary encounter with a giant serpent, which earned him his famous nickname. The story of Tawara Tōda is one of the most enduring and beloved in Japanese folklore, and it is often told as a tale of how an ordinary man, through his bravery and kindness, can achieve extraordinary feats and earn the favor of the gods and mythical beings.

The most famous episode in Tawara Tōda's legend begins with his encounter with the giant serpent. According to the tale, Hidesato was traveling along the shores of Lake Biwa, Japan's largest freshwater lake, when he came upon a massive serpent blocking the bridge he needed to cross. This serpent was no ordinary creature; it was the guardian of the lake, a supernatural being known as a dragon or ryū. The serpent was so enormous that its body stretched across the entire length of the bridge, preventing anyone from passing.

While most people would have been terrified at the sight of such a creature, Hidesato remained calm and unafraid. He approached the serpent with confidence and, rather than attacking or fleeing, he simply stepped over its body and continued on his way. This act of fearlessness and respect impressed the serpent, which transformed into a beautiful woman. The woman revealed herself to be the daughter of the Dragon King, the ruler of the underwater realm of Lake Biwa.

The Dragon King's daughter explained that she had been sent to test the courage of mortals because her family was in dire need of assistance. She told Hidesato that a giant centipede, known as *omukade*, had been terrorizing the underwater palace of the Dragon King and that none of the dragon's warriors had been able to defeat it. The centipede was an enormous and malevolent creature that posed a grave threat to the dragon's realm. The Dragon King had heard of Hidesato's bravery and hoped that he might be able to defeat the centipede.

Moved by her plight, Hidesato agreed to help. The Dragon King's daughter led him to the entrance of the underwater palace, where Hidesato was welcomed with great honor. He was provided with a magical bow and arrows, which were said to have been blessed by the gods and were the only weapons capable of piercing the tough hide of the omukade. Armed with these divine weapons, Hidesato waited for the centipede to appear.

When the omukade finally emerged from its lair, it was an awe-inspiring sight. The creature was said to be so large that it coiled around the mountains surrounding Lake Biwa, and its eyes glowed with a malevolent red light. Hidesato, undeterred by the centipede's terrifying appearance, took aim with his bow and fired an arrow at the creature. The first arrow struck the centipede but had no effect. Hidesato then realized that the centipede was protected by powerful magic and that ordinary arrows would not harm it.

Recalling a piece of ancient wisdom, Hidesato licked the tip of his next arrow and prayed for divine assistance before taking another shot. This time, the arrow struck true, piercing the centipede's eye and killing it instantly. The giant creature writhed in agony before finally collapsing into the lake, where it sank beneath the waves, never to be seen again. The Dragon King's palace was saved, and Hidesato was hailed as a hero.

In gratitude for his bravery, the Dragon King rewarded Hidesato with a number of magical gifts. Among these were a bottomless rice bale (from which he derived his nickname "Tawara Tōda"), a self-replenishing roll of silk, and an inexhaustible cooking pot. These gifts ensured that Hidesato and his descendants would never want for food, clothing, or sustenance. The rice bale, in particular, became a symbol of abundance and prosperity, and Hidesato's nickname, Tawara Tōda, became synonymous with his heroic deeds and the blessings he received.

Tawara Tōda's legend is significant for several reasons. First, it underscores the theme of the hero's journey, a common motif in mythology, where a protagonist must overcome great challenges with the help of supernatural forces. Hidesato's encounter with the serpent, his battle with the omukade, and the rewards he received reflect the archetypal narrative of a hero who is tested, triumphs over evil, and is ultimately blessed by the gods.

Second, the story emphasizes the importance of courage and respect in the face of the unknown. Hidesato's fearlessness and his willingness to step over the serpent without hesitation demonstrate a profound trust in his own abilities and in the natural order of the world. His actions suggest that true bravery involves not just physical strength, but also a calm and composed mind that can assess and respond to challenges without fear.

The gifts that Hidesato receives at the end of his journey also carry symbolic meaning. The bottomless rice bale, in particular, represents the concept of abundance and the idea that those who act with courage and honor will be rewarded with prosperity. In Japanese culture, rice is more than just a staple food; it is a symbol of life, fertility, and the blessings of the gods. By providing Hidesato with an inexhaustible supply of rice, the Dragon King acknowledges his valor and ensures that his family will be blessed for generations.

Tawara Tōda's story highlights the connection between the human world and the supernatural. The interaction between Hidesato and the Dragon King's daughter reflects the belief that the natural world is inhabited by powerful, often benevolent, spirits who can influence human affairs. The cooperation between Hidesato and these spirits reinforces the idea that harmony between humans and the supernatural is essential for the well-being of the world.

Chapter Three: Monsters and Mythical Creatures

Oni - The Demons of Japan

The word "oni" in Japanese can be translated as "demon" or "ogre," but these creatures are more complex than the simple Western idea of a devil. Oni have a long and varied history that reflects different aspects of Japanese cosmology and religious thought. In many ways, oni embody the human fear of the unknown, the unpredictable forces of nature, and the consequences of immoral behavior. The exact origin of the oni is difficult to pinpoint, as their characteristics evolved over time through influences from indigenous Shinto beliefs, Buddhism, and even Chinese and Indian mythology.

In Shinto, the indigenous religion of Japan, spirits and deities are deeply connected to nature. Both benevolent and malevolent spirits are believed to inhabit the natural world, and oni, in some cases, are thought to be malevolent spirits or deities who have fallen from grace. They represent the chaotic and destructive forces that exist outside the orderly human world. Early depictions of oni in Shinto belief may have reflected natural disasters like earthquakes, floods, or storms, which were attributed to angry spirits. As such, oni became symbols of disorder and destruction, often serving as harbingers of calamity.

Oni also became closely associated with the concept of hell and punishment in Buddhist cosmology, which was introduced to Japan around the 6th century. In Buddhist mythology, oni serve as enforcers of punishment in the underworld, or Jigoku, where they torture the souls of the wicked. This association with hell gave oni a more specific role as agents of moral consequence, punishing those who had committed grave sins during their lives. Stories about oni in Buddhist contexts often emphasize the consequences of immoral behavior, making these demons instruments of cosmic justice.

In terms of appearance, oni are typically depicted as large, grotesque, and humanoid creatures. They often have brightly colored skin, usually red, blue, or green, and are marked by sharp claws, wild hair, and a set of sharp horns protruding from their heads. Some have three eyes or multiple limbs, emphasizing their supernatural nature. Oni typically carry heavy clubs, known as kanabō, which symbolize their immense physical power and capacity for violence. In some versions, they wear loincloths made from the pelts of wild animals, further emphasizing their primal, untamed essence.

The physical characteristics of oni are often exaggerated to convey their otherworldly strength and ferocity. Their terrifying appearance is meant to instill fear, but oni are also frequently portrayed as slow-witted and easily outwitted by clever humans. This duality—of being immensely powerful yet intellectually deficient—gives oni a multifaceted role in Japanese folklore, making them both fearsome and, at times, comic figures.

One of the most famous stories involving oni is the legend of Shuten-dōji, a demon lord who terrorized the region around Mount Ōe. According to the tale, Shuten-dōji was once a human who, through indulgence in alcohol and evil behavior, became an oni. He gathered a group of followers and took over a mountain stronghold, where he would kidnap women and wreak havoc on nearby villages. The emperor, desperate to stop Shuten-dōji's reign of terror, sent the legendary samurai Minamoto no Yorimitsu, also known as Raikō, and his retainers to defeat the demon. Disguised as mountain priests, Raikō and his men infiltrated Shuten-dōji's lair and tricked him into drinking poisoned sake. After the oni fell into a drunken stupor, Raikō and his retainers beheaded him, bringing an end to his tyranny. The story of Shuten-dōji emphasizes the destructive potential of oni, but also the belief that cleverness and bravery can triumph over evil, no matter how powerful.

While oni are often portrayed as antagonistic figures in Japanese folklore, their role is not always strictly evil. In some cases, oni can be seen as protective spirits or deities that guard sacred places. In remote areas, local folk traditions sometimes view oni as guardians of mountain shrines or as the embodiment of natural forces that, while fearsome, are necessary for the balance of the world.

Despite their fearsome reputation, oni have also taken on a more playful role in modern Japanese culture. They frequently appear in festivals, particularly during the annual Setsubun festival, which marks the beginning of spring. During this festival, people throw roasted soybeans outside their homes while shouting "Oni wa soto, fuku wa uchi!" which means "Demons out, good fortune in!" This ritual is intended to drive away evil spirits and invite good luck for the coming year. In this context, oni serve as symbols of misfortune or bad luck, and the act of expelling them is a way for communities to cleanse themselves of negativity.

In modern popular culture, oni continue to be a common feature in anime, manga, video games, and other forms of media. Their menacing appearance and association with the supernatural make them compelling villains, but oni are also sometimes reimagined as misunderstood or even heroic characters.

Dragons in Japanese Mythology

Unlike their Western counterparts, which are frequently portrayed as malevolent and destructive, dragons in Japanese mythology are generally considered protective and wise, though they can be fierce when provoked. The image of the Japanese dragon is heavily influenced by Chinese mythology, from which much of Japan's early dragon lore is derived. In contrast to the fire-breathing dragons of European legend, Japanese dragons are typically depicted as long, serpentine creatures with no wings but possessing immense strength and control over water. They are said to have the ability to summon rain, storms, and floods, reflecting the dragon's close connection to the sea and the weather. Japanese dragons are usually depicted with scales, a long, sinuous body, and features resembling a combination of different animals, such as the head of a camel, the antlers of a deer, the claws of an eagle, and the whiskers of a catfish. These composite features underscore the dragon's role as a creature that transcends the ordinary boundaries of nature, embodying the power of many different life forms.

One of the most significant dragons in Japanese mythology is Ryujin, the dragon king of the sea. Ryujin is an ancient deity who rules over the vast oceanic realm from his underwater palace known as Ryugu-jo. This palace is often described as a magnificent structure made of coral, crystals, and precious stones, where Ryujin and his family reside. Ryujin is often depicted as a majestic dragon with immense power over the seas and its creatures, but he can also transform into human form when interacting with mortals.

Ryujin's connection to the sea places him at the heart of many myths that deal with water, weather, and the balance of the natural world. As the dragon king, Ryujin controls the tides, the waves, and the currents, and he is often invoked by sailors and fishermen who rely on his favor for safe passage and a bountiful catch. In agricultural communities, Ryujin's ability to control rain and storms also made him an important figure, as his powers were believed to influence the success of crops and harvests. As such, Ryujin was both feared and respected, a deity whose wrath could bring floods and destruction, but whose favor ensured prosperity and sustenance.

One of the most famous myths involving Ryujin is the story of how he provided the legendary warrior Empress Jingū with the tide jewels, or kanju and manju. According to the legend, during Empress Jingū's campaign to conquer the Korean peninsula, Ryujin gave her the magical tide jewels, which had the power to control the tides. When Jingū's forces were pursued by enemy ships, she threw the kanju into the sea, causing the tides to recede and stranding the enemy's vessels. As the enemy tried to flee, Jingū threw the manju, which raised the tides and drowned the enemy fleet. This myth not only illustrates Ryujin's dominion over the seas but also underscores the dragon's role in aiding Japan's imperial expansion and the divine protection of the Japanese state.

Ryujin also plays a central role in the tale of the fisherman Urashima Taro. In this story, Urashima Taro saves a turtle from harm, only to discover that the turtle is a servant of Ryujin. As a reward, the fisherman is taken to Ryugu-jo, the palace of the dragon king, where he is treated to a life of luxury. After spending what seems like a few days in the palace, Urashima Taro decides to return to his village. However, upon his return, he discovers that many centuries have passed in the human world. The story of Urashima Taro is one of the most famous folktales in Japan, and it reflects Ryujin's mysterious nature as a guardian of time and space, as well as his ability to blur the boundaries between the mortal world and the divine realm.

While Ryujin is perhaps the most well-known dragon in Japanese mythology, he is not the only one. There are other notable dragons that appear in various legends, often playing protective or destructive roles depending on the context. For example, the dragon Yamata no Orochi is a fearsome, eight-headed serpent that appears in the myth of the storm god Susanoo. According to the legend, Yamata no Orochi terrorized the land and demanded the sacrifice of young maidens. Susanoo, the exiled brother of the sun goddess Amaterasu, encountered the dragon when he came to earth and devised a plan to defeat it. With the help of the local people, Susanoo prepared eight vats of sake, which he used to intoxicate the dragon. Once the creature was incapacitated, Susanoo beheaded Yamata no Orochi, freeing the land from its reign of terror. In the process, he discovered the legendary sword Kusanagi, which was found in one of the dragon's tails and later became one of the three sacred treasures of Japan's imperial regalia.

In contrast to the destructive nature of Yamata no Orochi, other dragons are seen as protectors of specific regions or landmarks. For example, the legend of Kuzuryu, or the Nine-Headed Dragon, tells of a dragon that lived in a lake near Mount Fuji. Initially feared for causing floods and devastation, Kuzuryu was eventually pacified through religious rituals, and the dragon became a guardian deity of the region. This dual nature of dragons—capable of both destruction and protection—mirrors the unpredictable and often contradictory forces of nature they represent.

Dragons in Japanese mythology are also closely connected to Buddhist thought, where they serve as protectors of the Dharma (the teachings of the Buddha) and the natural world. In Buddhist cosmology, dragons are seen as benevolent beings who guard sacred places, such as temples and monasteries. These dragons are often depicted as wise and compassionate, in contrast to the fearsome image they sometimes hold in other stories. In some traditions, dragons are believed to have the ability to bring rain, and prayers to dragons are made during times of drought.

Tengu: The Mountain Spirits

The origin of the tengu can be traced to a combination of native Shinto beliefs and influences from Chinese and Indian mythology. The word "tengu" is thought to have originated from the Chinese term tiangou, meaning "heavenly dog," which referred to a meteorological phenomenon or a celestial spirit. Early depictions of the tengu in Japan were influenced by this Chinese concept, but over time, the tengu transformed into a uniquely Japanese figure with distinct characteristics and roles. In their early representations, tengu were viewed as disruptive and dangerous demons who caused natural disasters, such as storms or landslides, and who led people astray in the mountains. Their mischievous and often harmful behavior earned them a reputation as tricksters and harbingers of chaos.

One of the defining features of tengu is their appearance. Tengu are typically depicted in two forms: the karasu-tengu (crow tengu) and the yamabushi-tengu (mountain priest tengu). The karasu-tengu, which is considered the earlier and more primitive form, has the body of a human but the head and wings of a bird, specifically a crow. This birdlike appearance emphasizes the tengu's connection to nature and their ability to fly, symbolizing their freedom from the constraints of the human world. Karasu-tengu are often associated with wildness and primal forces, reflecting the untamed and unpredictable nature of the mountains they inhabit.

The yamabushi-tengu, on the other hand, resembles a human more closely, but with exaggerated features such as a long nose and fierce, glaring eyes. The yamabushi-tengu takes its name from the yamabushi, the ascetic mountain priests of the Shugendō tradition, who practiced rigorous spiritual and physical discipline in the remote mountains of Japan. These tengu are often depicted wearing the robes and carrying the staff of a yamabushi, highlighting their connection to the spiritual practices of the mountains. The long nose of the yamabushi-tengu is one of its most iconic features, and it has become a symbol of the tengu's proud and often arrogant nature.

Despite their fearsome appearance and reputation, tengu are not purely malevolent beings. In many stories, tengu are portrayed as protectors of the mountains and the forests. They are believed to guard sacred places, such as temples and shrines, as well as the natural environment. Tengu are deeply connected to the idea of the kami (spirits) that inhabit all things in Shinto belief, and their role as guardians aligns with the Shinto reverence for nature. In this capacity, tengu are often seen as protectors of pilgrims and travelers who show respect for the mountains, offering guidance to those who are lost or in need of help. However, they can also be harsh and unforgiving, punishing those who disrespect sacred spaces or who disturb the natural balance of the environment.

At the same time, tengu are notorious for their trickster behavior. They are known to play pranks on humans, leading them astray in the mountains, creating illusions, or causing confusion. These tricks can range from harmless mischief, such as stealing food or belongings, to more dangerous acts, such as leading travelers into perilous situations. The duality of tengu as both protectors and tricksters reflects the belief that the natural world is both nurturing and dangerous, offering blessings to those who respect it but punishing those who disregard its power.

Tengu also have a close association with martial arts, particularly the art of swordsmanship. In many legends, tengu are depicted as master warriors who possess unparalleled skill in combat. They are said to live in secluded mountain fortresses where they practice and refine their martial techniques. Tengu are often portrayed as teachers who impart their knowledge of swordsmanship and other martial skills to humans, but they are highly selective in choosing their students. Only those who are deemed worthy, either through their spiritual discipline or their bravery, are taught by the tengu. Some of Japan's most famous legendary warriors, such as Minamoto no Yoshitsune, are said to have been trained by tengu in the ways of the sword. These stories reflect the tengu's role as both spiritual and physical guides, offering their wisdom to those who are willing to learn but also testing the resolve of their students.

In some stories, tengu are depicted as enemies of Buddhism, seeking to disrupt the spiritual practices of monks and leading them into temptation or ruin. This antagonistic relationship is thought to stem from the tengu's association with pride and arrogance, traits that are antithetical to Buddhist teachings of humility and detachment. In these stories, tengu often appear as corrupt monks or as spirits who challenge the faith of Buddhist practitioners, reflecting the tension between the worldly desires represented by the tengu and the spiritual discipline of the monks.

Tengu have also become central figures in Japanese festivals and rituals, particularly those associated with the changing of seasons or the honoring of nature spirits. Masks of tengu with their long noses and fierce expressions are commonly used in theatrical performances and celebrations, symbolizing the presence of these powerful spirits in the human world.

Kitsune – The Fox Spirits

The origins of kitsune myths in Japan can be traced back to ancient times, and their development has been influenced by both native Shinto beliefs and imported Chinese and Indian folklore. Foxes have been present in Japanese culture for centuries, and over time, their image evolved into something more mystical. In Shinto, kitsune are closely associated with the kami Inari, the deity of rice, agriculture, fertility, and prosperity. Inari's messengers are said to be white foxes, and these foxes are viewed as sacred beings, entrusted with protecting the kami's shrines and ensuring the well-being of farmers and the land.

Inari shrines across Japan often feature statues of foxes, usually holding symbolic items such as a key (representing the storage of rice) or a jewel (symbolizing wealth and good fortune). Kitsune in this context are protectors, watching over the shrines and their visitors. They serve as intermediaries between the human and divine worlds, acting as guides or guardians. Inari's kitsune are particularly associated with rice and agriculture, reflecting the fox's ability to control or influence the fertility of the land.

One of the most distinctive traits of kitsune is their ability to shapeshift, a power they share with other spirits in Japanese mythology, such as tanuki (raccoon dogs). Kitsune are said to be able to transform into human form, most commonly that of a beautiful woman or an elderly man. The ability to shapeshift is believed to grow stronger as the kitsune ages; an older fox, particularly one that has lived for 100 years or more, is considered a master of transformation. Kitsune are also believed to grow additional tails as they age, with the most powerful kitsune having up to nine tails. These multi-tailed kitsune are called kyūbi no kitsune (nine-tailed foxes) and are considered to possess immense power, wisdom, and magical abilities.

The reasons behind a kitsune's shapeshifting vary across stories. In many cases, kitsune take on human form to interact with people, often with the goal of deceiving or playing tricks on them. These tricks can range from harmless pranks to more serious manipulations. In some stories, a kitsune may disguise itself as a young woman to seduce a man, only to later reveal its true nature and leave the man in confusion or distress. These tales often serve as cautionary stories about the dangers of being deceived by appearances and the unpredictability of the supernatural world.

However, not all stories of kitsune in human form are negative. There are numerous legends where a kitsune assumes a human identity out of love or compassion. In some cases, a kitsune falls in love with a human and lives with them for years, often without the human realizing their spouse's true identity. One of the most famous examples of this type of story is the tale of the kitsune-tsuki, or fox possession, where a man unknowingly marries a kitsune disguised as a woman. The couple lives happily together until the kitsune's true nature is discovered, usually after many years and the birth of children. In these stories, the kitsune often leaves the human world once its secret is revealed, but the bond between the fox spirit and the human remains, with the kitsune sometimes continuing to protect its former family from afar.

In other stories, kitsune serve as loyal and protective companions. A person who treats a kitsune kindly might receive its favor and protection for life. Kitsune are said to repay acts of kindness with blessings of good fortune, wealth, or success. This relationship between humans and kitsune can be deeply reciprocal, reflecting the belief that spirits, like humans, respond to how they are treated. In this protective role, kitsune often act as guardians, warding off evil spirits or bad luck, and guiding their human friends to safety.

Despite their capacity for protection, kitsune are also known for their mischievous and trickster nature. Their intelligence and cunning allow them to outwit humans, and they delight in causing confusion or playing pranks. These tricks can be harmless or, in some cases, malicious. Kitsune might lead travelers astray in the wilderness, causing them to become lost, or create illusions that confuse or deceive those around them. In some tales, kitsune create phantom fires, known as kitsune-bi, to lure people into dangerous situations. These fox-fires are said to be magical flames that light up the night, leading unsuspecting travelers into swamps, forests, or other treacherous places.

One of the more sinister aspects of kitsune lore involves possession, known as kitsunetsuki. In these stories, a kitsune enters a person's body, usually through the mouth, and takes control of their actions. Kitsunetsuki was once considered a real phenomenon in Japan, particularly in rural areas, and was thought to be the cause of strange behavior or illness. People believed that a kitsune could possess a person, often a young woman, causing her to act erratically or speak in strange voices. Exorcisms and rituals were performed to drive out the fox spirit, which was seen as a malevolent force. This association with possession reflects the ambivalence surrounding kitsune in Japanese culture—they are not inherently evil, but their powers make them both feared and revered.

Kappa – The River Children

Kappa are typically described as small, humanoid creatures with features that blend human and reptilian characteristics. They are usually depicted as about the size of a child, with green, scaly skin, webbed hands and feet, and a turtle-like shell on their backs. One of their most distinctive features is the dish-like depression on the top of their heads, called a sara, which holds water and is believed to be the source of their power. As long as the water in this dish remains intact, the kappa retains its strength and magical abilities. If the water is spilled or dried out, however, the kappa becomes weakened or immobilized, rendering it harmless.

The association of kappa with water is central to their identity. In traditional Japanese belief, water is both a life-giving force and a potential danger, capable of sustaining crops and communities but also bringing floods and other disasters. Kappa, as water spirits, embody this duality. They are often seen as protectors of their watery domains but are also capable of causing harm to those who disrespect or encroach on their territory. This relationship with water connects kappa to the Shinto belief in kami, or spirits that inhabit natural elements, making them a symbol of the need to respect nature's power.

One of the most famous characteristics of the kappa is its mischievous nature. Kappa are notorious for playing pranks on humans, particularly those who venture too close to rivers or lakes. These pranks can range from harmless to more serious in nature. For instance, kappa are known to peek up women's kimonos, steal crops, or playfully wrestle with humans. They are also famous for tricking travelers by imitating human voices or leading them into the water. In some stories, they knock over fishermen's boats or pull swimmers underwater for fun. These mischievous acts highlight the playful but potentially dangerous side of the kappa.

However, not all kappa encounters are benign. Kappa are also known for their darker tendencies, particularly their penchant for dragging people—especially children—into the water and drowning them. In some tales, kappa are even said to feed on humans, specifically targeting the shirikodama, a mythical organ believed to be located inside the victim's rectum. The shirikodama is thought to contain a person's soul, and the kappa's desire to extract it is often interpreted as a metaphor for the dangers lurking in deep waters or the fear of drowning. These darker elements of kappa folklore served as cautionary tales, warning children to stay away from rivers and ponds, where drowning was a real and constant danger in rural Japan.

In fact, they are often portrayed as beings who can be reasoned with or even befriended, provided they are treated with respect. One of the most well-known ways to subdue a kappa is through the act of politeness. Kappa are said to be extremely courteous, and if a human bows to a kappa, the creature will instinctively bow back. This action causes the water in the kappa's head to spill out, thus weakening the kappa and allowing the human to escape or gain the upper hand. In some stories, a kappa who has been outwitted in this way will pledge loyalty to the person who tricked them, offering to help with tasks such as irrigation, fishing, or even healing, as kappa are believed to have medical knowledge.

Another way to appease a kappa is by offering it cucumbers, which are said to be the creature's favorite food. In some regions of Japan, it is customary to write the names of family members on cucumbers and toss them into rivers or lakes as offerings to the kappa, in exchange for the creature's protection. This practice underscores the idea that kappa, like many other spirits in Japanese folklore, are not inherently evil but are beings that can be negotiated with or pacified through respectful behavior and offerings.

Kappa have also been known to show gratitude when humans treat them with kindness. In some stories, a kappa who has been saved from a predicament—such as having its dish refilled with water after drying out—will repay the favor by using its supernatural strength to help the person with farm work or other tasks. These stories reflect the belief that even mischievous or dangerous spirits like kappa can be benevolent when treated with respect and understanding.

In some folklore, kappa are depicted as being knowledgeable about medicine, particularly bone setting, and are sought after by humans for their healing abilities. The idea that kappa possess medical knowledge may stem from their association with water, which in many cultures is linked to healing and purification.

The Four Sacred Beasts

In Japanese mythology, the Four Sacred Beasts, also known as the Four Symbols, represent the four cardinal directions and play a significant role in East Asian cosmology. These mythological creatures—Seiryu (the Azure Dragon of the East), Byakko (the White Tiger of the West), Suzaku (the Vermilion Bird of the South), and Genbu (the Black Tortoise of the North)—symbolize the natural elements, seasons, and cosmic forces. Their origins are deeply rooted in Chinese mythology and cosmology, particularly in the concept of the Wuxing (Five Elements) and the Chinese system of celestial guardians. These mythological creatures were eventually absorbed into Japanese cultural and religious thought, where they became important symbols in both Shinto and Buddhist traditions, as well as in art, architecture, and folklore. They are believed to be powerful protectors, each guarding their respective direction and offering cosmic balance. They are also associated with seasons, colors, elements, and virtues, creating a complex system of symbolism that reflects the harmony between the natural world, the spiritual realm, and human life.

Seiryu, The Azure Dragon of the East

Seiryu is associated with the East, spring, and the element of wood, embodying renewal, growth, and the life-giving powers of water. The image of the dragon, particularly in East Asian traditions, differs greatly from its Western counterpart. In Japanese and Chinese mythology, dragons are revered as benevolent, wise, and powerful creatures, often linked to the natural elements, especially water, and associated with prosperity, protection, and balance. Seiryu, as the Azure Dragon, is a prime example of this symbolism, representing the dynamic energy of nature, the passage of seasons, and the eternal cycle of life.

As the guardian of the East, Seiryu is associated with the beginning of the day (since the sun rises in the east), as well as with the dawn of the year, signified by spring. The East, in this context, represents renewal, vitality, and rebirth—qualities that are reflected in Seiryu's role as a protector of the forces that drive natural growth and life. Spring, as the season of planting and regeneration, parallels the dragon's connection to water and fertility. Seiryu is thought to control the rains, which are essential for agriculture and the cycle of life, and in some legends, the dragon is credited with bringing rain to nourish crops and ensure prosperity.

The element of wood, which Seiryu governs, is another critical aspect of his role in Japanese mythology. Wood is associated with growth, flexibility, and strength, and in the ancient system of the Five Elements (Wu Xing)—a concept that underpins much of East Asian cosmology—wood stands for life, expansion, and the dynamic force that drives all living things. Just as trees grow from small seeds into mighty, towering forms, Seiryu's association with wood symbolizes the potential for growth, strength, and the unfolding of life's possibilities. This association is particularly important in an agrarian society where the prosperity of crops and nature's cycles determine survival.

Seiryu's physical form is that of a traditional East Asian dragon, a long, serpentine creature with scales and the ability to fly despite lacking wings. This iconic image of the dragon emphasizes Seiryu's connection to water, the heavens, and the earthly realms simultaneously. Dragons in East Asian mythology are not fire-breathing destroyers as they are often portrayed in Western mythologies; rather, they are associated with wisdom, strength, and guardianship, serving as intermediaries between the celestial forces and the natural world. Seiryu's ability to control water and bring rain ties him to the natural cycles that sustain life on Earth. In this sense, Seiryu is not just a force of protection but also a benefactor who ensures the well-being and prosperity of those under his care.

One of the most prominent cultural representations of Seiryu in Japan can be found in Kyoto at Kiyomizu-dera, a famous Buddhist temple. According to local legend, the temple is protected by a blue dragon believed to be Seiryu. The temple even hosts an annual festival, the Seiryu-e, or "Blue Dragon Festival," in which a large dragon puppet is paraded through the streets to honor Seiryu and invoke the dragon's protective power. The dragon is considered a guardian of the temple and the surrounding area, ensuring the safety of its inhabitants and protecting them from harm. This reflects Seiryu's role as a guardian deity, a creature that watches over the eastern quarter of the sky and maintains cosmic harmony.

Seiryu's association with protection is also evident in his connection to warriors and martial traditions. In both Japanese and Chinese culture, dragons symbolize power, authority, and the ability to overcome adversity. As a guardian of the East, Seiryu is often invoked in protective rites or rituals to ward off evil spirits and to ensure the success of important ventures. In this role, Seiryu exemplifies the protective and benevolent nature of dragons in Japanese mythology—beings that guard against chaos and disorder, ensuring peace and prosperity through their influence over natural and spiritual realms.

Seiryu's presence extends beyond religious and mythical texts into various art forms, including painting, sculpture, and architecture. Many traditional Japanese buildings and temples feature images of Seiryu, especially on gates and doorways, symbolizing the dragon's role as a guardian who watches over the structure and the people who enter it. In this context, Seiryu is often depicted as a coiled, majestic dragon, its sinewy form stretching across walls or curling around pillars, a symbol of protection and divine presence.

Byakko, The White Tiger

Byakko governs the West, symbolizing autumn, the element of metal, and the color white. His role within Japanese mythological cosmology is closely linked to balance and harmony, particularly in the interplay between the natural and celestial realms.

The association with autumn is significant because it reflects Byakko's role as both a harbinger of change and a protector of what has been cultivated. In East Asian cosmology, autumn represents the season when life begins to contract, following the flourishing of spring and summer. It is a time of harvesting and storing what the earth has produced, symbolizing both the end of a growth cycle and the preparation for the cold, dormant months ahead. Byakko, as the guardian of the West, stands watch over this critical period of transition, ensuring that balance is maintained as the natural world enters a state of decline and eventual renewal.

In terms of the element of metal, Byakko's connection to this fundamental force further emphasizes his role as a figure of strength and discipline. Metal is associated with qualities such as resilience, sharpness, and structure. It represents the force that cuts through disorder and chaos, restoring order and protecting what is essential. Byakko's nature as a tiger aligns with these qualities, as tigers are creatures known for their power, precision, and dominance in the natural world. The element of metal, particularly in its symbolic association with autumn, also represents harvesting and cutting away what is unnecessary, which echoes the tiger's role in maintaining the balance between life and death, growth and decay.

Byakko's white color carries deep symbolic meaning in East Asian culture. White is the color of purity, but it is also associated with death and mourning in traditional

Japanese and Chinese beliefs. This dual symbolism reflects the ambivalence of Byakko's role: while he is a powerful protector and force for righteousness, his domain over the West and autumn also ties him to the natural process of decline and the inevitable end of life. In this way, Byakko embodies both the ferocity of nature and its solemn beauty, enforcing the cosmic order with a combination of strength and reverence for life's cycles.

One of the most enduring aspects of Byakko's mythological role is his association with military strength and martial valor. Tigers have long been revered as symbols of strength, ferocity, and the ability to overcome formidable challenges, qualities that are particularly prized in warrior cultures. Byakko, as the White Tiger, is often invoked in the context of war and protection, where his energy is thought to inspire bravery, justice, and the defense of righteousness. In many ways, Byakko serves as a celestial embodiment of the ideals of the samurai class, who valued honor, courage, and a sense of duty to protect the land and their people.

In Chinese mythology, which heavily influenced Japanese interpretations, Byakko's rise to his role as the guardian of the West is tied to the belief that the White Tiger would only appear when the world was governed by a just ruler or when there was peace throughout the land. This underscores the idea that Byakko is a symbol of order and cosmic balance, emerging in times of righteousness to ensure that justice is upheld. In Japan, this aspect of Byakko's myth translated into a symbol of moral strength, with the White Tiger often representing the idea that strength must be wielded with a sense of justice and moral clarity.

Byakko is frequently depicted in art, particularly in the form of statues, paintings, and carvings that adorn temples, shrines, and other sacred spaces. Often, Byakko is shown as a regal, powerful tiger, sometimes standing or crouching in a posture that conveys both readiness and calm authority. His white fur, which is depicted in stark contrast to his sharp, intense eyes, highlights his role as a figure of purity, strength, and vigilance. In Japanese temple iconography, Byakko's image may appear alongside those of Seiryu, Suzaku, and Genbu, symbolizing the protective power of the four celestial beasts working in harmony to maintain cosmic balance.

One notable cultural association with Byakko in Japan is his connection to protective rites, particularly those performed for warriors and military leaders. In ancient times, Byakko's energy was often invoked to ensure victory in battle and to protect soldiers from harm. His fierce, yet controlled power was seen as the ideal force to inspire courage and discipline among fighters. In some regions, talismans or amulets bearing the image of Byakko were used to ward off evil spirits or to protect individuals from physical and spiritual dangers.

Suzaku, The Vermilion Bird

Suzaku, often depicted as a phoenix-like bird, is not merely a symbol of fiery destruction but embodies the dual nature of fire: its capacity for both devastation and renewal. In Japanese and East Asian mythology, Suzaku is a revered guardian of the southern direction and represents not only the heat and brilliance of the summer sun but also the dynamic energy of life, transformation, and spiritual enlightenment.

Suzaku is sometimes seen as a symbol of rebirth and renewal, much like the phoenix that rises from its own ashes. This symbolism reflects the idea that destruction is often a precursor to new beginnings, a theme central to the concept of fire in myth and religion. Just as fire burns away the old to make way for the new, Suzaku's energy is one of purification and transformation, suggesting that endings and destruction are necessary steps in the cycle of life.

As the guardian of the South, Suzaku represents the peak of the sun's power, corresponding to the height of summer when the days are longest and the heat of the sun is at its most intense. The direction of the South, in East Asian cosmology, is linked to warmth, growth, and prosperity, qualities that Suzaku embodies in both its fiery nature and its connection to life's generative forces. Summer, as the season of abundance and activity, is associated with the flourishing of crops and the full vitality of nature. Suzaku's presence as the guardian of this season underscores its role in ensuring the balance of life's cycles—growth in the summer must eventually give way to the harvest in autumn and the dormancy of winter.

Suzaku's association with fire also ties it to the concept of purification. In many cultures, fire is seen as a cleansing force, capable of destroying impurities and transforming the physical world into something purer. In Japanese and Chinese religious traditions, fire is often used in rituals to ward off evil spirits, cleanse spaces, or purify the body and mind. Suzaku, as the embodiment of fire, serves as a celestial protector, capable of burning away negativity and evil. This aspect of Suzaku's symbolism is not only limited to physical fire but also extends to the metaphorical and spiritual fire within—the passion, energy, and clarity needed to overcome obstacles and achieve spiritual growth.

Fire is both a creative and destructive force, and Suzaku's role as a guardian reflects the importance of maintaining harmony between these two aspects. The brilliance and heat of fire are necessary for life and growth, but uncontrolled fire can also bring destruction. Suzaku represents the balance between these forces, ensuring that the energy of fire is used constructively rather than destructively. In this way, Suzaku is not only a protector of the physical world but also a symbol of inner balance and discipline.

The image of Suzaku can often be found in temples, shrines, and other sacred spaces, particularly in the form of statues, paintings, or carvings that honor the Four Sacred Beasts. Suzaku's fiery red plumage and dynamic, birdlike form make it a popular subject in Japanese art, where it is often depicted alongside its fellow celestial guardians, each watching over their respective directions. In Buddhist and Shinto practices, Suzaku is sometimes invoked as a protector, particularly in rituals meant to purify spaces, ward off evil, or bring balance and harmony to the environment.

One notable site in Japan where Suzaku is honored is the southern gate of Heian Shrine in Kyoto, which is dedicated to the Four Sacred Beasts. The southern gate, known as Suzakumon, is named after Suzaku and symbolizes the protection offered by the Vermilion Bird. The presence of Suzaku at such sites reflects its continued importance in Japanese culture as a symbol of protection, balance, and renewal.

Suzaku's role in Japanese cosmology also has a close relationship with the concept of onmyōdō, an ancient Japanese system of divination and cosmology influenced by Taoism, Buddhism, and Shintoism. In onmyōdō, the Four Sacred Beasts, including Suzaku, play an important role in maintaining the balance of the universe through their respective elemental and directional associations. Suzaku's connection to fire, summer, and the South helps to maintain the harmony of natural forces, ensuring that the cosmos remains in balance and that life on Earth continues to flourish according to the proper cycles.

Genbu, The Black Tortoise

Genbu, associated with the North, symbolizes winter, the element of water, and the color black. What makes Genbu particularly unique among the Four Sacred Beasts is its dual nature, often depicted as a combination of two animals—a tortoise entwined with a snake. This complex symbolism, which integrates ideas of strength, endurance, and wisdom, gives Genbu a distinct place in East Asian cosmology, where it represents the steady, protective force of the northern direction.

The tortoise, as a core part of Genbu's form, carries deep symbolic meaning in both Japanese and broader East

Asian culture. Tortoises are often associated with longevity, stability, and resilience due to their long lifespans and hard shells. In many traditions, they are seen as creatures that embody the enduring forces of the natural world, representing the slow but steady progress of time. In the context of Genbu's association with winter, the tortoise can be seen as a symbol of endurance through harsh conditions, as winter is a season of dormancy and survival. Just as the tortoise withdraws into its shell for protection, Genbu embodies the qualities of preservation and the ability to endure and protect through difficult periods.

The inclusion of the snake, which is often depicted coiling around the tortoise in artistic renderings of Genbu, adds another layer of symbolic meaning. Snakes are frequently associated with transformation, regeneration, and adaptability due to their ability to shed their skins. This dual symbolism—combining the steady, enduring nature of the tortoise with the transformative energy of the snake—makes Genbu a creature that represents both stability and the potential for change. In this way, Genbu embodies the balance between constancy and transformation, a reflection of the cyclical nature of the seasons and the rhythms of life itself.

Genbu's association with the element of water further reinforces these ideas. Water is a powerful symbol in Japanese mythology, representing life, purity, and the flow of energy, but it also has connotations of depth, mystery, and danger. As the guardian of the North, Genbu is linked to the cold, life-sustaining properties of water in winter, a time when rivers and lakes may freeze over, but also a time when water is stored and preserved for future use. Water's ability to adapt to different forms—liquid, solid, and vapor—mirrors the tortoise and snake's symbolic combination of stability and transformation, with water taking on different states depending on the conditions it encounters.

Winter, the season associated with Genbu, is another key aspect of its symbolism. Winter is a time of rest, reflection, and endurance in many cultures, marking the end of the natural cycle before the renewal of spring. In East Asian cosmology, winter's association with the North and Genbu suggests a period of dormancy, where life is preserved rather than active, waiting for the right conditions to flourish again. This reflects Genbu's protective nature, as winter serves as a time of hibernation and conservation, where resources are carefully managed to ensure survival. Genbu, as the protector of this period, embodies the wisdom and patience needed to endure difficult times, making it a symbol of resilience and long-term strength.

In terms of color symbolism, black, the color associated with Genbu, carries a variety of meanings in Japanese and East Asian thought. While black is often seen as a color of mystery, the unknown, and even death, it also represents depth, the unseen forces of the universe, and the potential for renewal. In Japanese culture, black can signify authority and formality, qualities that resonate with Genbu's role as a guardian and protector. It is a color that suggests seriousness and a connection to the deeper forces of nature, including the cycle of death and rebirth that Genbu represents through its association with winter and water.

As the Sacred Beast of the North, Genbu is responsible for watching over and defending the northern direction, both in the physical and spiritual realms. This protective role is mirrored in religious practices, where images of Genbu are often placed at the northern gates of temples or shrines, symbolizing its ability to ward off evil spirits and ensure the safety of the sacred space. In Chinese Daoism, Genbu (Xuanwu) is sometimes depicted as a warrior deity, further reinforcing its association with protection and martial strength. In Japan, Genbu's presence in religious and cultural symbolism reflects the broader East Asian belief in the importance of balance, order, and protection in the cosmos.

One of the most famous cultural associations with Genbu in Japan can be found in Kyoto, where the northern gate of the ancient city was traditionally guarded by Genbu. Genbu's image often appears in temple iconography, alongside the other Three Sacred Beasts—Seiryu, Byakko, and Suzaku—each guarding their respective directions and helping maintain cosmic order.

Chapter Four: The Underworld and Otherworldly Realms

Afterlife in Japanese Mythology

The afterlife in Japanese mythology is a complex and multifaceted concept shaped by a blend of Shinto beliefs, Buddhist teachings, and folk traditions. Japanese perspectives on death and the afterlife reflect the country's cultural and spiritual diversity, weaving together indigenous notions of purity, ancestral veneration, and the cycles of nature with imported ideas from Buddhism, such as reincarnation and karmic consequence.

In Shinto, Japan's indigenous religion, the afterlife is most commonly associated with Yomi, the Land of Darkness. Yomi is a shadowy realm where the spirits of the dead reside in a state of eternal stasis, cut off from the world of the living. Unlike many other religious traditions where the afterlife might offer a form of judgment or reincarnation, Yomi is not a place of reward or punishment; rather, it is a neutral realm where death represents impurity and separation from the natural cycle of life. Once a soul enters Yomi, it cannot return to the living world, and its state of existence is one of decay and stagnation.

The concept of Yomi is best illustrated in the Shinto creation myth, where the god Izanagi descends into Yomi to retrieve his deceased wife, Izanami. Izanami, after dying during childbirth, had become a resident of Yomi, transforming into a decayed and corrupted figure. Izanagi's attempt to bring her back is thwarted by the irreversible nature of death, symbolized by the corruption of her body and the decay inherent in Yomi itself. When Izanagi flees from Yomi, pursued by the vengeful spirits of the underworld, he ultimately seals the entrance to Yomi with a large boulder, marking a clear boundary between the realms of the living and the dead.

This myth highlights the Shinto understanding of death as a state of impurity, or kegare, which contrasts with the purity and vitality of life. In this view, the dead must be kept separate from the living to avoid contamination. This belief has deeply influenced Shinto practices surrounding death, including purification rituals, funeral customs, and the treatment of ancestral spirits. While Yomi is not a place of torment, it represents the inevitable and permanent divide between life and death, and the transition to Yomi marks the end of one's participation in the living world.

Despite the grim nature of Yomi, Shinto also emphasizes the importance of ancestor worship and the continued presence of spirits in the natural world. Deceased ancestors are often venerated as kami, or spiritual beings, who continue to influence the lives of their descendants. Through rituals, offerings, and festivals, the living maintain a relationship with the spirits of their ancestors, seeking their protection and guidance. This practice of honoring the dead reflects a more positive view of the afterlife, where the spirits of the deceased are not confined solely to Yomi but can exist in the form of protective kami who remain connected to the living world.

Buddhism, introduced to Japan in the 6th century, brought with it a more elaborate vision of the afterlife, emphasizing reincarnation, karma, and multiple realms of existence. In Buddhist cosmology, the cycle of death and rebirth, known as samsara, is governed by the law of karma, where one's actions in life determine the nature of their next existence. Good deeds lead to more favorable rebirths, while negative actions result in suffering in the next life. The ultimate goal in Buddhism is to escape the cycle of samsara and achieve enlightenment, or nirvana, which represents liberation from the endless cycle of death and rebirth.

In Japan, Buddhist beliefs about the afterlife were adapted to complement existing Shinto and folk practices, leading to a syncretic view of death and the beyond. The idea of Jigoku, or Buddhist hell, became an important part of Japanese eschatology. Jigoku is a place of suffering where souls who have committed serious misdeeds are sent to atone for their sins. In contrast to Yomi, which is a neutral and passive realm, Jigoku is a place of active punishment, overseen by the fearsome Enma, the king of hell. Enma judges the souls of the dead and determines their fate based on the karma they accrued during their lives. Those sent to Jigoku must endure various torments, depending on the nature of their sins, until they have paid for their transgressions and can be reincarnated into a new life.

Buddhism also introduced the concept of Pure Land (Jōdo), an idealized paradise where souls could be reborn through devotion to the Buddha Amida (Amitabha). Pure Land Buddhism, which became especially popular in Japan, offered the promise of rebirth in this blissful realm for those who sincerely recited the name of Amida Buddha.

The Pure Land was seen as a stepping stone toward ultimate enlightenment, providing a safe haven from the suffering of samsara. This vision of a peaceful afterlife where one could eventually achieve nirvana was appealing to many, especially in times of social or political unrest, and it offered a more optimistic view of what could await the soul after death.

In addition to Shinto and Buddhist concepts of the afterlife, Japanese folklore is rich with tales of ghosts and spirits, known as yurei, who remain trapped between the worlds of the living and the dead. Yurei are often portrayed as restless souls who are unable to find peace due to unfinished business, strong emotions like anger or jealousy, or improper funerary rites. These spirits linger in the mortal world, sometimes haunting specific places or people. Stories of yurei are common in Japanese literature and theater, such as the famous ghost story of Oiwa from the kabuki play Yotsuya Kaidan, in which a wronged woman returns as a vengeful spirit to seek retribution.

The presence of yurei in Japanese folklore reflects anxieties about death and the proper treatment of the dead. It was believed that failing to perform the necessary funeral rituals or disrespecting the dead could lead to their spirits returning to cause harm. As a result, there is a strong emphasis on ensuring that the deceased are honored appropriately, both through funeral rites and ongoing practices of ancestor worship. By maintaining this connection with the dead, it is believed that their spirits can find peace and continue to protect the living as benevolent ancestors.

Ne-no-Kuni – The Root Country

While Yomi is traditionally seen as the primary destination for the dead in Shinto belief, Ne-no-Kuni represents a different kind of underworld, one that is more closely associated with the ancestral roots of the gods and an extension of the earth's natural forces. Though less frequently mentioned than Yomi, Ne-no-Kuni occupies a significant place in Japan's mythological landscape, where it symbolizes the mysterious connection between life, death, and the cyclical nature of existence.

The idea of Ne-no-Kuni appears in both the Kojiki (Records of Ancient Matters) and the Nihon Shoki (Chronicles of Japan), two foundational texts of Japanese mythology compiled in the 8th century. It is connected to the earth, the roots of plants, and the ancestral origins of the kami (gods), suggesting that this underworld is more closely tied to the cycles of nature than Yomi's realm of darkness and death.

One of the most significant mentions of Ne-no-Kuni is in the story of Ōkuninushi. Ōkuninushi, whose name means "Great Land Master," is a god associated with the earth, agriculture, and nation-building. His adventures and trials take him through various realms, including Ne-no-Kuni, which is described as the domain of his ancestral god, Susanoo, the storm god and brother of Amaterasu, the sun goddess.

The journey of Ōkuninushi to Ne-no-Kuni is a key part of his myth. After suffering numerous betrayals by his brothers, who repeatedly attempt to kill him out of jealousy, Ōkuninushi escapes to Ne-no-Kuni seeking refuge and wisdom. There, he meets Susanoo and undergoes a series of trials to prove his worth. Susanoo's tests of strength and wit symbolize the challenges that Ōkuninushi must overcome in order to establish himself as a rightful ruler and protector of the land. These trials, however, also mark Ne-no-Kuni as a place of transformation and renewal—a realm where challenges are faced and power is gained, contrasting with the hopeless inertia of Yomi.

Ne-no-Kuni, in this context, serves as a place where deities reconnect with their roots, draw strength from the earth, and renew their purpose. Unlike Yomi, which is often portrayed as a destination of finality where spirits are trapped in eternal decay, Ne-no-Kuni appears as a place of ancestral power, where gods return to the source of their divine heritage. After passing Susanoo's trials and marrying his daughter Suseri-hime, Ōkuninushi gains the wisdom and authority needed to ascend as the ruler of the earthly realm. This victory highlights the importance of Ne-no-Kuni as a space for growth and empowerment, rather than simply a destination for the dead.

The name "Ne-no-Kuni" itself carries deep symbolic meaning. The word "ne" refers to roots, as in the roots of plants or the foundational origins of things. In this way, Ne-no-Kuni can be understood as the "Root Country," a place where life's origins, both physical and spiritual, are grounded. This association with roots evokes a sense of continuity, as the roots of a tree are what sustain life and growth above ground. Ne-no-Kuni, therefore, symbolizes a connection to the ancient, enduring sources of life and creation, making it a more generative and transformative space than Yomi, which represents death's finality.

In some interpretations, Ne-no-Kuni is also linked to fertility, agriculture, and the cycles of life, death, and rebirth. The connection between Ne-no-Kuni and the roots of plants suggests that this underworld is tied to the forces that sustain life, rather than merely ending it. Ōkuninushi, as the god of agriculture and land, embodies this life-sustaining aspect, and his journey to Ne-no-Kuni reflects his role as a deity who bridges the worlds of the living and the dead, the above and the below, through his mastery over the land and its resources.

It is also worth noting that Ne-no-Kuni's role in Japanese mythology, particularly as seen through Ōkuninushi's journey, reflects broader Shinto beliefs about the interconnectedness of the natural and spiritual worlds. In Shinto, life and death are not strictly opposing forces but are part of a larger, cyclical process that encompasses all existence. The gods themselves, through their own trials, deaths, and rebirths, mirror the natural rhythms of the earth, reinforcing the idea that death is not an end but a transition within a greater, cosmic order. Ne-no-Kuni's symbolic connection to the roots of life underscores this concept, reminding us that death, like the roots of a tree, is part of the cycle that sustains life.

Despite its significance in the myth of Ōkuninushi, Ne-no-Kuni is not as well developed in Japanese mythology as other realms like Yomi or Takamagahara. However, its place in Shinto cosmology provides a valuable contrast to these other worlds, emphasizing the diversity of perspectives on life, death, and the afterlife within Japanese religious thought. Ne-no-Kuni, with its associations with roots, growth, and transformation, offers an alternative vision of the underworld—one that is less about the end of life and more about the continuous connection between past, present, and future, between the gods and the land, and between the living and their ancestral roots.

Takamagahara – The High Plain of Heaven

Takamagahara is the celestial realm of the gods in Japanese mythology. It serves as the home of the kami, the deities worshipped in Shinto, and is the divine counterpart to the mortal world. The concept of Takamagahara originates in the Kojiki (Records of Ancient Matters) and the Nihon Shoki (Chronicles of Japan), two of the earliest written accounts of Japanese mythology and history, compiled in the 8th century. These texts lay out the structure of the cosmos, presenting Takamagahara as a realm that exists far above the earthly plane, known as Ashihara no Nakatsukuni (the Central Land of Reed Plains), where humans reside. While Ashihara no Nakatsukuni represents the mortal world of impermanence and struggle, Takamagahara is portrayed as a place of divine purity, order, and power, inhabited by the kami who influence all aspects of creation and life.

Takamagahara is often depicted as a place of light, peace, and divine authority, a contrast to the darker, more chaotic realms like Yomi (the Land of the Dead) or Ne no Kuni (the Land of Roots), which are associated with death and decay. In Shinto belief, the separation between Takamagahara and the world of humans is fundamental, yet permeable, with gods occasionally descending to the mortal realm or communicating with humans through rituals, oracles, and natural phenomena. Similarly, mortals can seek the favor or intervention of the gods through prayer, offerings, and festivals, which are believed to strengthen the connection between Takamagahara and Ashihara no Nakatsukuni.

One of the most important deities in Takamagahara is Amaterasu, the sun goddess and arguably the most revered figure in Shinto mythology. Amaterasu is often considered the supreme deity of Takamagahara, governing the sun and providing light to both the heavens and the mortal realm. As the progenitor of the imperial family, Amaterasu's divine authority serves as the foundation for the legitimacy of the Japanese emperor, who is believed to be her direct descendant. The mythological connection between the emperor and Takamagahara reinforces the notion that the imperial family serves as a bridge between the divine world and the human realm, linking the mortal world to the sacred order of the gods.

The most well-known myth involving Amaterasu and Takamagahara is the story of the sun goddess retreating into a cave after being offended by her brother, Susanoo, the storm god. According to the legend, Susanoo's destructive behavior and disrespect drove Amaterasu to withdraw from the heavens and hide herself in a cave, plunging both Takamagahara and the earthly world into darkness. The absence of Amaterasu's light created chaos among the gods, and the balance of nature was disrupted. In an effort to coax her out of the cave, the other gods gathered outside and performed a raucous ritual involving music, dance, and laughter. This spectacle eventually drew Amaterasu's curiosity, and when she peered out of the cave to see what was happening, she was lured out with the help of a mirror. Once she emerged, the sun's light returned to both the heavens and the earth, restoring order and balance.

This myth highlights several key aspects of Takamagahara and its role in the cosmos. First, it underscores the importance of harmony among the gods, as the well-being of the celestial realm directly affects the earthly realm. It also reflects the belief that the balance between natural forces, symbolized by the relationships among the gods, is essential for the continuation of life on earth. The actions of the gods in Takamagahara are not isolated but have direct consequences for the mortal world.

Takamagahara also plays a significant role in the myth of the descent of Ninigi, the grandson of Amaterasu, to earth. This event, known as Tenson kōrin (the "Descent of the Heavenly Grandson"), marks the establishment of divine rule over the human world. According to the myth, Amaterasu sent Ninigi from Takamagahara to Ashihara no Nakatsukuni with the divine mandate to govern the land and bring order to the earthly realm. Ninigi's descent was accompanied by the presentation of the three sacred treasures—Kusanagi no Tsurugi (the sword), Yata no Kagami (the mirror), and Yasakani no Magatama (the jewel)—which symbolized the divine authority and legitimacy of the imperial line. These treasures, which remain part of the Japanese imperial regalia today, serve as a direct connection between the imperial family and

Takamagahara, reinforcing the idea that the emperor is a living representative of the gods.

This myth not only establishes the divine origins of the Japanese imperial family but also illustrates the hierarchy within Takamagahara itself. The kami of Takamagahara are organized into a celestial court, with Amaterasu often seen as the supreme ruler. Other important deities, such as Tsukuyomi, the moon god, and Susanoo, the storm god, also inhabit this heavenly realm, each with their own distinct roles and domains. The relationships among these gods, both cooperative and antagonistic, reflect the natural cycles of creation, destruction, and renewal that govern the world.

The gods of Takamagahara are believed to intervene in human affairs when necessary, offering protection, blessings, and guidance to those who honor them through rituals and devotion. Shrines dedicated to the gods serve as physical manifestations of this connection, where people can pray for divine favor or express gratitude for the gods' protection.

The Myth of Mount Fuji

Standing at 3,776 meters (12,389 feet), Mount Fuji is revered as a sacred mountain, deeply associated with both Shinto and Buddhist beliefs. Its majestic form is seen as a gateway between the human world and the divine, embodying the power of nature, the impermanence of life, and the pursuit of enlightenment.

The spiritual significance of Mount Fuji is rooted in ancient Shinto beliefs, where mountains are often regarded as sacred spaces inhabited by the spirits of nature, known as kami. In Shinto cosmology, kami are believed to reside in natural features such as trees, rivers, and mountains, making Mount Fuji one of the most important and powerful sacred sites in Japan. The mountain is seen as the dwelling place of powerful deities who govern over the natural and spiritual realms. For many centuries, it has been a place of pilgrimage, with devotees climbing its slopes in the belief that ascending the mountain brings them closer to the divine.

One of the most important deities associated with Mount Fuji is Konohanasakuya-hime, the goddess of Mount Fuji and the symbol of delicate earthly life. Her name translates to "Princess Blossoming like Flowers," and she is often depicted as a goddess of both beauty and fragility, with her power linked to nature's cycles of growth and decay.According to mythology, Konohanasakuya-hime married the god Ninigi-no-Mikoto, the grandson of the sun goddess Amaterasu. Together, they represent the divine ancestry of the Japanese imperial family. Konohanasakuya-hime's role as the protector of Mount Fuji adds to the mountain's spiritual allure, as many believe she watches over the area, safeguarding those who climb its slopes and offering blessings of fertility, protection, and beauty.

The most famous myth surrounding Mount Fuji is the legend of its creation. According to an ancient folktale, Mount Fuji was formed in a single night. The myth recounts how a large earthquake struck the land, and when the earth trembled and shook, a massive hole was created, which filled with the waters to become Lake Biwa, Japan's largest freshwater lake. The earth that had been displaced during the creation of the lake rose into the sky and formed Mount Fuji.

Another important myth associated with Mount Fuji involves the story of Taketori Monogatari (The Tale of the Bamboo Cutter), one of Japan's oldest and most beloved folktales. In this story, a bamboo cutter discovers a tiny, radiant princess named Kaguya-hime inside a bamboo stalk. As Kaguya-hime grows, she becomes renowned for her beauty, and many suitors seek her hand in marriage. However, she reveals that she is not from this world but from the moon, and she must eventually return to her celestial home. Before leaving, she gives the emperor of Japan a letter and an elixir of immortality. Heartbroken by her departure, the emperor orders that the letter and the elixir be burned at the highest mountain in the land, which was Mount Fuji. According to the legend, the smoke from this fire rose from the peak and continues to this day, symbolizing the mountain's connection to the heavens and the divine. The name "Fuji" is said to derive from the word fushi or fuji, which means "immortal," further solidifying Mount Fuji's role as a symbol of eternity and divine presence.

Mount Fuji's sacred status is also reinforced by its prominence in Buddhist beliefs, particularly within the tradition of Fujiko, a mountain-worshipping sect that flourished during the Edo period (1603–1868). Followers of Fujiko believed that Mount Fuji was a living entity, the embodiment of the Buddha, and a site for achieving enlightenment. The practice of climbing Mount Fuji became a religious ritual, with devotees undertaking arduous pilgrimages to ascend the mountain as an act of purification and spiritual awakening. The journey up the mountain was seen as a metaphor for the path toward enlightenment, with the peak representing nirvana or ultimate spiritual clarity. For these pilgrims, reaching the summit was not merely a physical achievement but a sacred journey toward spiritual rebirth.

The Buddhist influence on Mount Fuji is also evident in the concept of thc "Three Holy Mountains" of Japan, which includes Mount Fuji, along with Mount Haku and Mount Tate. These mountains are regarded as sacred sites where the physical and spiritual worlds intersect, and where the presence of the divine is most strongly felt. For centuries, Buddhist monks and ascetics have climbed Mount Fuji, seeking to tap into its spiritual power and meditate at its peak, which they believe is a place where the boundary between the material and spiritual realms is thin.

Mount Fuji's connection to the Buddhist tradition is further symbolized by its representation of Fuji Sengen, a syncretic deity worshipped at the Sengen shrines that dot the mountain's base and summit. The Sengen shrines are dedicated to Konohanasakuya-hime, but they also reflect the blending of Shinto and Buddhist beliefs, where the mountain is revered as both a home of the gods and a site for spiritual transformation. Pilgrims visit these shrines to offer prayers for protection before beginning their ascent, reinforcing the belief that Mount Fuji is a conduit between the earthly and the divine.

The famous ukiyo-e artist Katsushika Hokusai's series of woodblock prints, Thirty-Six Views of Mount Fuji, immortalized the mountain in Japanese art, capturing its majesty and spiritual resonance from various perspectives. Even today, Mount Fuji is a popular destination for climbers and pilgrims alike, with thousands ascending its slopes each summer, continuing the tradition of reverence and spiritual seeking that has surrounded the mountain for centuries.

Chapter Five: Regional Myths and Folktales

Tales from Okinawa and the Ryukyu Islands

Okinawa and the Ryukyu Islands, located in the southernmost part of Japan, possess a rich and distinct cultural heritage, separate from that of mainland Japan. These islands, with their unique history and geography, were home to the independent Ryukyu Kingdom until their incorporation into Japan in the late 19th century. This cultural separation has preserved a wealth of indigenous myths and folklore that differ significantly from the more familiar stories of Japanese Shinto or Buddhist traditions. The myths of Okinawa and the Ryukyu Islands are deeply tied to the sea, the islands' natural environment, and the ancestors, reflecting both the geographical isolation of the region and its historical connections to Southeast Asia, China, and Japan.

One of the most important and pervasive themes in Ryukyuan mythology is the worship of ancestral spirits, particularly in the form of kami and kami-asagi, or sacred spaces dedicated to these spirits. Unlike the highly formalized shrines of Shintoism on the mainland, Okinawan sacred sites are often more closely tied to the natural landscape—groves, beaches, caves, and springs that are considered imbued with spiritual energy. This reflects a broader animistic belief system where nature itself is seen as alive and filled with spirits. The reverence for ancestors is central to Okinawan spirituality, and many myths revolve around the relationship between the living and the dead, with rituals intended to honor the spirits of ancestors, who are believed to continue influencing the world of the living.

One of the central figures in Ryukyuan mythology is Amamikyu (or Amamiko), a goddess regarded as the creator of the Ryukyu Islands and the ancestral mother of its people. According to legend, Amamikyu was sent from the heavens by the supreme deity to create the Ryukyu Islands. She descended to Earth and molded the islands from the primordial chaos of the sea. Amamikyu is also said to have brought life to the islands, creating humans and teaching them how to live in harmony with nature. As the progenitor of the Ryukyu people, she holds a revered place in their spiritual traditions, and her legacy is honored at many sacred sites across the islands, including Sefa-utaki, a highly venerated place of worship that served as a center for Ryukyuan religious ceremonies.

The mythology surrounding Amamikyu not only highlights the Ryukyu people's reverence for the natural world but also their deep connection to the sea. The islands' dependence on the ocean for survival is reflected in many other myths, where the sea serves as both a life-giving force and a source of danger. One such example is the tale of the nirai kanai, a mythical paradise believed to exist far beyond the horizon, across the ocean. In Ryukyuan cosmology, nirai kanai is a place from which all life and blessings come, including fertile land, bountiful harvests, and favorable weather. The people of the Ryukyus believe that spirits from nirai kanai occasionally visit the islands, bringing gifts of abundance and prosperity.

This belief in nirai kanai reflects the islanders' spiritual connection to the sea and the idea that the ocean is a bridge between the earthly world and the divine. Ceremonies and rituals are often performed to honor the spirits of nirai kanai, particularly during times of planting and harvest, as the islanders seek to maintain a harmonious relationship with these benevolent forces. At the same time, the sea's destructive potential is also acknowledged, with storms and rough seas sometimes interpreted as the anger of spirits displeased by human actions.

One of the most well-known deities tied to the sea in Ryukyuan mythology is Ryūjin, the dragon god of the ocean. While Ryūjin is also known in mainland Japanese mythology, his role in the Ryukyu Islands takes on special significance due to the maritime nature of the culture. Ryūjin is seen as a powerful, shape-shifting deity who rules over the seas, controlling storms, waves, and tides. Fishermen and sailors would offer prayers and sacrifices to Ryūjin to ensure safe voyages and bountiful catches. Temples dedicated to Ryūjin are found across the Ryukyu Islands, and his influence over the sea and its creatures highlights the crucial role of the ocean in the islanders' way of life.

Women play a particularly important role in Ryukyuan spiritual life. Female shamans, called noro or yuta, are central figures in the religious practices of the islands, conducting ceremonies and serving as the caretakers of sacred spaces. The importance of women in the spiritual hierarchy is tied to the belief that women have a special connection to the gods and spirits, as well as the ancestral world. This matriarchal aspect of Ryukyuan spirituality is one of the features that sets it apart from both mainland Japanese Shinto and other East Asian religious practices.

Another unique aspect of Ryukyu mythology is the presence of shisa, the lion-dog guardian spirits. Shisa, which are often depicted as statues placed at the entrance of homes, temples, and other buildings, are said to protect against evil spirits and bring good fortune. The belief in shisa is thought to have been influenced by Chinese guardian lions, but the Ryukyu version is distinct in its form and symbolism. Shisa are usually depicted in pairs, with one having an open mouth (to ward off evil spirits) and the other with a closed mouth (to keep good spirits inside). These protective creatures are emblematic of the syncretic nature of Ryukyuan religion, blending local animistic traditions with influences from mainland China and Japan.

The myths and spiritual beliefs of the Ryukyu Islands reflect the region's unique geographical and cultural history, emphasizing the interconnectedness of the people with their natural surroundings, particularly the sea. The creation myths, like those of Amamikyu, place a strong focus on the land's divine origins, while tales of nirai kanai and Ryūjin highlight the deep respect and reverence for the ocean. The role of female spiritual leaders, the belief in local kami, and the presence of shisa all contribute to a distinctive religious and mythological landscape that differentiates the Ryukyuan islands from the rest of Japan.

Ainu Mythology

Unlike the dominant Shinto and Buddhist traditions of mainland Japan, Ainu mythology evolved separately, maintaining its own distinct pantheon of gods and spirits, as well as unique creation myths that emphasize the symbiotic relationship between humans and the natural environment. The Ainu worldview is fundamentally animistic, where every aspect of the natural world, from rivers to mountains to animals, is imbued with spirits known as kamuy. These kamuy govern the forces of nature and play a central role in the daily lives and spiritual practices of the Ainu people.Among these, Kotan-kor-kamuy—the Creator god, whose name means "God of the Village"—is one of the most significant figures in Ainu creation stories. According to Ainu mythology, Kotan-kor-kamuy created the land and the people, and he continues to protect the Ainu people, ensuring their survival through the provision of food and natural resources. The myths describe him as a benevolent god who acts as a caretaker of the Ainu, providing the means for their existence and guiding them in their interactions with the natural world.

One of the most revered kamuy in Ainu mythology is Kim-un-kamuy, the god of bears and mountains. The bear, or kim-un-kamuy, holds a special place in Ainu culture, as it is regarded not just as an animal but as a physical manifestation of a powerful deity. The Ainu believe that the bear is a gift sent from the heavens, a divine being temporarily living in the form of an animal. Central to Ainu ritual life is the iyomante, or bear ceremony, where a bear is ritually hunted, captured, and eventually sacrificed as an offering to Kim-un-kamuy. The Ainu see this as returning the bear spirit to the kamuy, expressing gratitude for the animal's sacrifice, which provides the community with food and materials. This ceremony underscores the Ainu's deep reverence for nature and their understanding of the interconnectedness of life and death, where hunting and the consumption of animals are seen as part of a sacred exchange between humans and the gods.

The Ainu also have creation myths that explain how the world was formed and how humans came to inhabit it. One prominent myth tells of the origins of the earth through the actions of the fire goddess Apehuchi-kamuy and her sibling, Kando-koro-kamuy, the god of thunder. Apehuchi-kamuy, who governs fire and the hearth, is a central figure in the household and in Ainu religious practice. She is believed to protect homes and families, and her spirit resides in the hearth, which is the focal point of the Ainu home. In Ainu cosmology, fire plays a dual role: it is both a life-giving force that sustains humans and a spiritual entity that connects them to the divine.

In one version of the Ainu creation myth, Apehuchi-kamuy descends to Earth from the upper world, accompanied by Kando-koro-kamuy, to prepare the world for human habitation. Together, they shape the land, making it suitable for life, and Apehuchi-kamuy teaches the people how to use fire, which becomes central to their survival and spiritual practice. The creation of the world is not a singular event but a process that requires the cooperation of multiple kamuy, each contributing their specific powers to bring about balance and harmony. In this sense, Ainu mythology reflects the belief that the world is maintained through an ongoing relationship between humans, animals, and the spirits of the natural world.

Another essential figure in Ainu mythology is Repun-kamuy, the god of the sea, who is responsible for the fish and other marine life that sustain the Ainu people, who traditionally relied heavily on fishing. Repun-kamuy governs the waters, ensuring that the sea is bountiful, but he is also a capricious deity who can unleash storms and rough seas when he is angered or disrespected. To ensure the goodwill of Repun-kamuy, the Ainu offer prayers and rituals before setting out to fish, asking for his protection and favor. The relationship between the Ainu and Repun-kamuy reflects the broader Ainu belief in the importance of respecting the natural forces and deities that provide sustenance, as well as the need to maintain harmony with these powerful forces.

In addition to the major deities, Ainu mythology is populated with a variety of spirits and creatures that interact with humans, often as helpers or protectors. Among these are the koropokkuru, small, mythical beings believed to live beneath the roots of trees or in burrows in the ground. According to legend, the koropokkuru were the original inhabitants of the land before the Ainu arrived. They are depicted as kind and generous, sometimes helping the Ainu by leaving food and tools for them, but they are also elusive, rarely revealing themselves to humans. In some stories, humans and koropokkuru lived in harmony, but the relationship deteriorated when humans began to take advantage of the koropokkuru's kindness. The myth of the koropokkuru underscores themes of reciprocity, respect, and the consequences of human greed.

The Ainu also hold a belief in the ramat, or soul, which is present in all living things, including humans, animals, plants, and even inanimate objects. In Ainu cosmology, the soul is eternal and does not perish with the body. After death, the soul travels to the land of the dead, known as kotan ne ramat, where it continues to exist. The Ainu believe that maintaining a respectful relationship with the spirits of the deceased is essential for ensuring the continued well-being of the living. This belief in the interconnectedness of all living things, through their shared possession of a soul, reflects the animistic foundation of Ainu spirituality.

The Ainu relationship with nature is one of reciprocity, where humans are expected to respect and honor the spirits that provide them with food, shelter, and protection. In return, the gods ensure that the land remains fertile, the seas bountiful, and the harmony between the human and spiritual realms intact.

Kyushu Legends

Kyushu, the third-largest island in Japan and the southernmost of the country's four main islands. This terrain, marked by both beauty and danger, plays a central role in shaping the myths and legends of the region. Many of Kyushu's stories revolve around volcanic activity, natural phenomena, and the powerful kami (gods or spirits) who are believed to influence the forces of nature.

One of the most prominent and awe-inspiring natural features of Kyushu is Mount Aso, the largest active volcano in Japan and one of the largest calderas in the world. Mount Aso's volcanic activity has long been a source of both fear and reverence for the people of Kyushu, and many myths have arisen to explain its destructive power. In Shinto, natural phenomena like volcanoes are believed to be the manifestations of kami, and Mount Aso is no exception. The mountain is said to be home to Aso-no-kami, a powerful deity who controls the volcanic forces within the mountain.

According to one of the most well-known legends, Aso-no-kami was originally a protective god who watched over the region, ensuring fertility and prosperity for the people. However, as the island experienced periods of turmoil and imbalance, the kami's wrath was unleashed in the form of volcanic eruptions. These eruptions were seen as divine punishments, warnings to the people that they had strayed from a path of respect for the natural world and the kami. To appease Aso-no-kami, the local population would perform rituals and offer sacrifices, seeking to restore harmony and prevent further destruction.

The mythology surrounding Aso-no-kami is both ancient and deeply interwoven with the spiritual practices of the people living around the volcano. The mountain itself is considered a sacred space, with Aso Shrine at its foothills serving as a place of worship for centuries. Aso-no-kami is believed to reside within the mountain, governing its eruptions and quelling its destructive forces when properly honored through rituals and offerings. Local legends tell of Aso-no-kami's role in shaping the land, often describing the god as a powerful force who tamed the wild fires of the volcano and transformed the region into a fertile, inhabitable place.

One of the most well-known legends associated with Mount Aso involves Takeiwatatsu-no-Mikoto, a heroic figure in Kyushu's mythological tradition who is credited with taming the violent volcanic forces of the region. Takeiwatatsu, said to be a descendant of Ninigi-no-Mikoto, the divine grandson of the sun goddess Amaterasu, is often depicted as a brave warrior who subdued a fire-breathing serpent or dragon that lived in the caldera of Mount Aso. This serpent, representing the raw, untamed power of the volcano, caused destruction across the land through its fiery breath and eruptions. By defeating the serpent, Takeiwatatsu helped to bring order to the region, allowing the people to settle and cultivate the land around Mount Aso.

The story of Takeiwatatsu's victory over the fire serpent reflects the broader theme in Japanese mythology of humans or gods working in harmony with nature to tame and balance its forces. In this context, Aso-no-kami, as the deity of Mount Aso, is not merely a god of destruction but also a protector who oversees the delicate balance between life and death, creation and destruction. The volcanic soil around Mount Aso is known for its fertility, and the region's agricultural success is often attributed to the blessings of Aso-no-kami.

Another aspect of Kyushu's volcanic mythology is the importance of hot springs, or onsen, which are abundant in the region due to its geothermal activity. The hot springs are seen as blessings from the volcanic kami, providing both physical healing and spiritual purification. These hot springs are often associated with water deities like Suijin, the god of water, who works in harmony with volcanic kami to create the life-giving springs. The combination of fire and water in Kyushu's mythology reflects the island's volcanic nature, where these opposing elements coexist to sustain life.

Tales from the Tohoku Region

The Tohoku region is located in the northeastern part of Japan's main island of Honshu. Known for its rugged landscapes, with mountains, forests, and harsh winters, Tohoku has nurtured a unique blend of mythology that reflects the region's isolation, natural beauty, and the challenges faced by its people. The folktales and myths of Tohoku are deeply rooted in animism, Shinto traditions, and Buddhist influences, but they also carry distinct local elements that set them apart from the myths found in other regions of Japan.

The mountainous terrain of the region is home to several sacred peaks, which are often believed to be inhabited by powerful kami. For instance, Mount Osore, located on the Shimokita Peninsula in Aomori Prefecture, is considered one of Japan's most sacred mountains. The mountain's otherworldly landscape, characterized by volcanic craters, sulfurous hot springs, and eerie silence, has long been associated with the afterlife. In local belief, Mount Osore is considered a gateway to the underworld, where souls of the dead are believed to reside. The Bodaiji Temple, which sits near Mount Osore's shores, is a place where people come to communicate with the spirits of their deceased loved ones, often with the help of mediums called itako. These blind female shamans act as intermediaries between the living and the dead, channeling the spirits of the departed and delivering messages to the living. This practice, unique to the Tohoku region, is a testament to the region's deep connection to both the spirit world and the natural landscape.

Another key figure in Tohoku mythology is Jizo Bosatsu, a bodhisattva who is revered as the protector of children, travelers, and the souls of the dead. While Jizo is venerated throughout Japan, in the Tohoku region, his presence is particularly strong due to the region's history of harsh winters, famine, and poverty. Statues of Jizo can be found in many rural villages, often standing near crossroads or in remote mountain passes, where they are believed to protect travelers from danger and guide lost souls to the afterlife. In many folktales from Tohoku, Jizo appears as a kind and compassionate figure who helps those in need, particularly children and the poor. The people of Tohoku traditionally make offerings to Jizo in the hope of securing his protection and blessings, and his gentle, guardian-like nature reflects the region's deep-rooted belief in the need for spiritual support in the face of hardship.

Tohoku is also known for its rich tradition of yokai—supernatural creatures and spirits that populate the region's folklore. One of the most famous yokai from the region is the Namahage, a fearsome ogre-like figure that plays a central role in an annual ritual held in Akita Prefecture. The Namahage, dressed in straw cloaks and wearing demonic masks, are said to descend from the mountains each New Year's Eve to visit villages and scare away evil spirits. In the ritual, the Namahage enter homes, shouting at the residents and demanding to know if there are any lazy or disobedient children in the household. This dramatic performance serves both as a moral lesson and a form of spiritual cleansing, as the Namahage are believed to chase away bad luck and bring blessings for the coming year. The Namahage tradition is one of Tohoku's most well-known cultural practices and reflects the region's unique blend of mythology, morality, and local beliefs.

Another notable yokai from Tohoku is the Zashiki-warashi, a mischievous spirit believed to inhabit homes, particularly in the Iwate Prefecture. Zashiki warashi are depicted as childlike figures, often invisible to adults but seen by children. While they are generally benevolent, Zashiki-warashi enjoy playing pranks and causing minor mischief around the house. However, their presence is considered a sign of good fortune, and it is said that households with a Zashiki-warashi will enjoy prosperity and happiness, while those who lose one will fall into decline. In many folktales, families go to great lengths to please the Zashiki-warashi, offering food or leaving toys for the spirit in hopes of keeping it content. The Zashiki-warashi myth highlights the importance of maintaining harmony with the spirit world, as well as the belief that supernatural beings can have a direct impact on everyday life.

The Tohoku region's folklore also features tales of kitsune (foxes) and tengu (bird-like mountain goblins), both of which are common throughout Japanese mythology but take on unique local forms in the northeastern region. Foxes, known for their shape-shifting abilities, are often depicted as tricksters in Tohoku folktales, capable of both helping and deceiving humans. In some stories, foxes transform into beautiful women to deceive men, while in others, they act as protectors of the forests and rice fields, symbolizing fertility and the power of nature. Tengu, on the other hand, are believed to inhabit the dense mountain forests of Tohoku, where they are said to possess supernatural strength and wisdom. In local myths, tengu sometimes teach humans secret martial arts or offer spiritual guidance, though they are also known for playing tricks on those who wander too deep into their territory.

Tohoku's folktales often reflect the harsh realities of life in the region, where people have long contended with difficult winters, natural disasters, and economic hardship. Stories of survival, resilience, and cooperation are common themes, as are tales that emphasize the importance of respecting nature and the spirits that dwell within it. For instance, legends of yama-no-kami (mountain deities) are widespread in Tohoku, where the mountains are seen as both protectors and sources of danger. The yama-no-kami are believed to control the natural resources of the mountains, including the game and fish that the people rely on for food. Hunters and fishermen in the region traditionally make offerings to the yama-no-kami to ensure successful harvests and avoid the wrath of the mountain gods.

Chapter Six: Legacy of Japanese Mythology

Japanese mythology has had a profound influence on modern popular culture, particularly in the realms of anime, manga, and contemporary storytelling. The themes, characters, and narratives from ancient mythological sources have found new life in these mediums, blending traditional beliefs with modern sensibilities.

One of the most direct ways in which mythology influences popular culture is through the adaptation of well-known deities and spirits into anime and manga. These mediums often feature characters inspired by Shinto and Buddhist figures, reinterpreted in ways that fit modern narratives. For example, Amaterasu, the sun goddess and one of the central figures in Shinto mythology, has been featured in various forms of media. In the video game Okami (2006), Amaterasu is portrayed as a divine wolf who must restore balance to the world by bringing light back to the land. While the game takes artistic liberties, the central concept of a divine being restoring order and fighting off chaos mirrors her role in traditional mythology as the source of life and order. Similarly, anime series such as Noragami feature modern depictions of lesser-known kami who navigate both the human world and the divine, offering new interpretations of their mythological roles.

The mythological theme of kami, or nature spirits, is prevalent in anime and manga, where these spirits are often shown interacting with the human world. Studio Ghibli's Princess Mononoke (1997), directed by Hayao Miyazaki, is a prominent example of how mythology is interwoven with environmental and moral themes. In the film, various forest spirits and gods, including the Forest Spirit (a clear reference to nature deities), fight to protect the natural world from human encroachment. The battle between the spirits of nature and industrial forces reflects not only an environmental message but also the deep respect for nature and the belief in the sacredness of the natural world that is central to Shinto. Miyazaki frequently draws on traditional Japanese beliefs about the interconnectedness of all life, and his works often feature characters, such as the kami or tengu, drawn from both mythology and folklore.

Another critical aspect of Japanese mythology found in popular culture is the concept of dual worlds or overlapping realities. In mythology, this is reflected in the existence of separate realms for gods, humans, and spirits—such as Takamagahara (the High Plain of Heaven) for the gods, and Yomi (the land of the dead) for deceased spirits. Modern anime and manga often explore this theme, with many stories involving characters who can travel between different worlds or dimensions. For instance, in Spirited Away (2001), a young girl enters a magical world populated by gods and spirits after wandering into a seemingly abandoned bathhouse. The idea of accidentally crossing into a realm where mythological creatures reside echoes traditional tales of humans interacting with the supernatural. Spirited Away masterfully captures the wonder and danger of the spirit world, much like traditional myths where mortals must navigate a delicate balance with powerful, otherworldly forces.

Monsters, demons, and supernatural creatures—commonly referred to as yokai in Japanese folklore—are another major influence on anime and manga. These creatures have been adapted into modern media in numerous forms. Anime like GeGeGe no Kitaro, which began as a manga in the 1960s, centers around yokai and their interactions with humans. Kitaro, the protagonist, is a yokai who defends humanity from more dangerous spirits, providing an example of how ancient folklore about supernatural beings has been reimagined to fit the superhero narrative popular in contemporary media.

Yokai like the tengu , oni (demons), and kitsune frequently appear in anime and manga, often retaining their traditional characteristics but placed in new contexts. Kitsune, for example, are shape-shifting fox spirits known in folklore for their ability to assume human form, often playing the role of tricksters or protectors. In modern manga and anime, kitsune often appear as complex characters with supernatural abilities, such as in the popular series Naruto, where the protagonist carries the power of the Nine-Tailed Fox, a mythological creature tied to kitsune folklore. These mythological creatures, while sometimes altered for modern storytelling, remain rooted in the traditional imagery and symbolism found in ancient Japanese tales.

The theme of reincarnation, central to Buddhist mythology, also plays a significant role in anime and manga. Reincarnation, along with the karmic cycles of death and rebirth, is a common plot device used to explore themes of fate, destiny, and moral consequences. Series such as Inuyasha (which draws heavily on Japanese folklore) often feature characters who are reincarnated or must deal with the karmic repercussions of past lives. In these stories, the idea of rebirth is used not only as a mythological reference but also as a narrative device that allows for complex character development and exploration of spiritual growth.

The modern Japanese fascination with transformation and the supernatural often stems from these ancient myths. Themes of personal change, as seen in many anime where characters grow stronger, assume new identities, or transcend their mortal limits, can be traced back to the mythological transformations of gods, spirits, and even humans in traditional stories. For example, the Shinto myth of Izanagi cleansing himself after his journey to the underworld and thereby creating new gods is mirrored in many stories where characters undergo purification or transformation after facing trials or entering dangerous, forbidden places.

Beyond direct references to deities and supernatural beings, Japanese mythology's influence on popular culture is also seen in the thematic exploration of morality, the balance between good and evil, and the consequences of disrupting natural harmony. The stories often center around the idea of harmony with nature, the importance of community, and respect for the unseen spiritual forces that govern the world. These themes, deeply ingrained in Shinto and Buddhist mythology, are woven into the fabric of modern storytelling in Japan, where protagonists frequently face moral dilemmas that challenge not only their personal ethics but also their relationship with the world around them.

Connections and Contrasts Between Japanese Myths and those of Other Cultures

By comparing Japanese myths with those from other traditions, such as Greek, Norse, or Hindu mythology, we can better understand how cultures across the world have grappled with the same fundamental questions—about creation, death, the gods, and humanity's place in the universe—while also developing unique interpretations shaped by their environments, histories, and spiritual beliefs.

One of the most fundamental areas of comparison is in creation myths. Most cultures possess some form of cosmogonic myth, explaining how the world and humanity came into being. In Japanese mythology, the creation story centers around the deities Izanagi and Izanami, who, according to the Kojiki and Nihon Shoki, created the Japanese islands by stirring the primordial ocean with a heavenly spear. Drops of water falling from the spear formed the first island, Onogoro, where Izanagi and Izanami descended to create the rest of Japan and the natural world. This process of creation from a primeval ocean can be seen in many other mythological traditions. For example, in the Babylonian creation epic Enuma Elish, the gods create the world by subduing the chaos of the primordial waters represented by the goddess Tiamat. Similarly, in Norse mythology, the world emerges from the chaos of the void known as Ginnungagap, with the first beings formed from the melting ice of Niflheim.

However, while Japanese and other myths often begin with chaos or a primordial sea, the role of the gods and the tone of the creation process differ significantly. Japanese creation myths place emphasis on harmony and balance, a reflection of Shinto's core values of living in accord with nature and maintaining equilibrium between the human, divine, and natural worlds. In contrast, many other mythologies emphasize conflict and struggle during the creation process. In Greek mythology, for example, the universe is born from a series of violent struggles, such as the overthrow of Uranus by his son Cronus, followed by Cronus's defeat by Zeus. The cosmic order in Greek myths is forged through violent contests of power, reflecting a more conflict-driven narrative of creation.

The relationship between gods and humans in Japanese mythology also contrasts with that found in other traditions. In Shinto, the kami—the spirits or gods—are not always distant, omnipotent beings. Rather, they are immanent in nature and can be found in rivers, mountains, animals, and even objects. The kami interact closely with humans, who honor them through rituals and festivals to maintain a harmonious relationship. This animistic view of the divine is paralleled in many indigenous traditions worldwide, such as the beliefs of Native American tribes or the animistic religions of Africa, where spirits reside in natural elements, and humans are seen as living in a web of interconnection with these spirits.

In contrast, the gods in other major traditions, such as in Greek or Hindu mythology, tend to exist in more distinct realms separate from the human world, interacting with mortals less frequently or under more extraordinary circumstances. In Greek mythology, the Olympian gods reside on Mount Olympus, and while they may intervene in human affairs, they are typically removed from the daily life of mortals. Similarly, in Hindu mythology, the gods exist in heavenly realms like Svarga, although they occasionally incarnate as avatars to intervene in human history, as seen with the god Vishnu's incarnations as Rama and Krishna.

Another key area of comparison is the underworld and conceptions of death. In Japanese mythology, the underworld is represented by Yomi, the land of the dead, which is described as a dark, stagnant realm where souls go after death. Yomi is a place of impurity, and once a soul enters, it is generally unable to leave. This bleak vision of the afterlife shares similarities with the Greek conception of Hades, the shadowy underworld where most souls reside in a state of quiet existence, neither suffering nor experiencing joy. However, in contrast to the intricate moral system of the Greek underworld, which includes different areas for the virtuous and the wicked (such as the Elysian Fields and Tartarus), Yomi lacks this division. There is no concept of reward or punishment in Yomi, reflecting a more neutral and perhaps somber view of death.

This conception also contrasts with the complex reincarnation system found in Hindu and Buddhist beliefs, where the cycle of rebirth (samsara) plays a central role in the afterlife. In these traditions, death is not the final resting place of the soul; instead, the soul is reborn in a new form based on its karma. In Japan, Buddhism was introduced in the 6th century and eventually blended with native Shinto beliefs. Over time, Buddhist ideas of reincarnation and the afterlife were incorporated into Japanese spirituality, creating a syncretic view that blends both the Shinto concept of Yomi and the Buddhist cycle of rebirth. This combination of views is uniquely Japanese and demonstrates how foreign religious ideas can intermingle with local beliefs to create a new mythological framework.

Another theme frequently found across mythologies is that of the heroic journey, which appears prominently in both Japanese mythology and in other cultural traditions. One of the most famous heroes in Japanese mythology is Yamato Takeru, a legendary prince known for his strength, bravery, and tragic fate. His exploits, such as taming wild lands and slaying enemies, bear a strong resemblance to the adventures of other mythological heroes like Heracles in Greek mythology or Gilgamesh in Mesopotamian mythology. Each of these heroes embarks on dangerous quests, battles fearsome creatures, and ultimately faces their mortality, often symbolizing humanity's struggle against the forces of chaos or fate.

However, there are important differences in how these heroes are portrayed. In Japanese mythology, Yamato Takeru's fate is deeply connected to the landscape and the kami. His journey reflects a moral lesson about the dangers of hubris and the need for humility and reverence toward the gods. In contrast, Greek heroes like Heracles often embody physical prowess and personal glory, with their tales emphasizing individual achievement and sometimes defiance of the gods. Similarly, the epic of Gilgamesh focuses on the hero's quest for immortality and his eventual acceptance of human limitations, a theme of existential reflection that resonates differently from Yamato Takeru's spiritually driven narrative.

Japanese mythology shares many common motifs with other global mythologies, such as creation from chaos, the presence of gods and spirits, the journey to the underworld, and the hero's quest. However, it is distinct in its emphasis on harmony with nature, the integration of Shinto and Buddhist beliefs, and its unique portrayal of the gods as immanent, closely linked to the natural world. While universal themes like life, death, and heroism are present across cultures, the way they are framed and understood in Japanese mythology highlights the cultural and religious values that have shaped Japan's spiritual landscape for centuries.

Recommendations for Further Study

For those who wish to deepen their understanding of Japanese mythology, several avenues of exploration will provide a more comprehensive insight into this rich and complex tradition. To explore its depths, it is important to study both primary sources and scholarly interpretations while engaging with cultural practices that preserve these ancient beliefs. Below are recommendations for further study:

1. Primary Texts: Kojiki and Nihon Shoki

A foundational step in the study of Japanese mythology is to engage with the primary sources that contain its earliest records. The **Kojiki** (Records of Ancient Matters) and the **Nihon Shoki** (Chronicles of Japan) are the two key texts where most of Japan's mythological narratives are documented.

- **Kojiki**: Written in 712 CE, the Kojiki is the oldest extant chronicle in Japan and contains the most detailed mythological accounts, including the creation myths, genealogies of deities, and stories of the kami. Translation by Donald L. Philippi is a widely respected English version, offering detailed annotations and cultural context.
- **Nihon Shoki**: Compiled in 720 CE, this text provides a more historical perspective on Japanese mythology. Its accounts are often more formal and include references to Chinese cosmology, showing the interaction of external influences with native beliefs. The English translation by W.G. Aston is the standard for English-speaking scholars.

Reading these texts in tandem allows for comparative analysis, providing insight into the evolving portrayal of myths, as well as the political and cultural motivations behind the recording of these stories.

2. Exploration of Shinto Practices

As mythology in Japan is deeply intertwined with Shinto, the indigenous religion, a study of **Shinto practices** is essential to understanding how myths are not just stories but living traditions. Engaging with the rituals, festivals, and shrines that honor the kami can provide a more visceral understanding of the beliefs and values that stem from these myths. Key recommendations include:

- **Visits to Sacred Sites**: Visiting Shinto shrines, particularly major sites such as **Ise Jingu** (dedicated to Amaterasu) or **Izumo Taisha** (associated with the deity Ōkuninushi), allows for direct engagement with spaces considered the earthly dwelling places of the kami. Many shrines hold festivals and ceremonies that embody the myths, such as the Shikinen Sengu, the periodic rebuilding of Ise Shrine, which reflects ancient cyclical beliefs.
- **Study of Shinto Rituals and Festivals**: Works like **"Shinto: The Kami Way"** by Sokyo Ono offer a readable introduction to Shinto beliefs and practices. More in-depth explorations can be found in books such as **"Shinto: A History"** by Helen Hardacre, which provides a comprehensive historical overview of the development of Shinto and its relationship to mythology.

3. Academic Analyses and Comparative Mythology

Scholarly works that analyze Japanese mythology through various lenses—such as anthropology, religious studies, or comparative mythology—can offer fresh perspectives and deeper critical engagement. Some key academic texts include:

- **"Japanese Mythology: Hermeneutics on Scripture and Narrative"** by Kazuo Matsumura is a detailed study on the interpretation of mythological texts and how they reflect Japanese cosmology, politics, and social structures.

- **"The Cambridge History of Japanese Religions"** offers multiple perspectives on how mythology interacts with religious practice, historical development, and political power, providing both context and a broader framework for understanding mythology's role in society.
- **"Comparative Mythology"** by Jaan Puhvel provides a comparative study of mythological themes across cultures, including Japan. This approach reveals cross-cultural similarities and differences, enriching the understanding of Japan's place within the global mythological landscape.

4. Art, Literature, and Performance

Japanese mythology has long inspired works of art, literature, and performance, offering another dimension of study through which myths have been interpreted and expressed. Several areas of focus can be fruitful for further exploration:

- **Noh and Kabuki Theatre**: Many traditional Noh and Kabuki plays are based on mythological themes, such as the stories of Yamato Takeru or the deities of heaven and earth. Watching these performances, or reading translations of key plays like **"The Tale of the Heike"**, provides insight into how myths have been dramatized and interpreted through performance arts.

- **Classical and Contemporary Art**: Japanese mythology has been depicted in classical ukiyo-e prints, such as those by artists like **Hokusai** and **Kuniyoshi**, and in modern media such as anime and manga. Books like **"The Art of Japanese Mythology"** by Christine Guth explore how visual arts have represented these stories, and how mythology continues to inspire contemporary Japanese pop culture.
- **Modern Interpretations in Anime and Manga**: Anime series such as **"Naruto"** or **"Princess Mononoke"** draw directly from mythological themes and characters, demonstrating the persistence of myth in modern storytelling. Studying these adaptations provides insight into how myths evolve over time and remain relevant in the contemporary Japanese imagination.

5. Cross-Cultural Mythological Studies

To fully appreciate the unique aspects of Japanese mythology, it is valuable to engage in comparative studies with other cultural mythologies, such as Chinese, Korean, or Ainu traditions, as well as more distant mythologies like those of Greece, Egypt, or Mesopotamia. This approach reveals both shared archetypal structures and distinct cultural expressions of myth.

"Mythologies of the World: A Comparative Guide" by Lincoln Kann delves into the comparative study of global myths, including Japan, and helps contextualize Japanese mythological themes within a broader mythological framework.

Afterword

The exploration of Japanese mythology opens a window into the rich spiritual and cultural heritage that has shaped Japan's identity for millennia. The myths, rooted in the land, reflect the strong connection between humanity and nature that lies at the heart of Shinto, Japan's indigenous religion, and this connection extends to almost every facet of Japanese life, from art and literature to religious practice and cultural festivals.

Throughout history, Japanese mythology has proven resilient, evolving as it absorbed foreign influences such as Buddhism and Confucianism, while remaining a cornerstone of the Japanese worldview. As we conclude this exploration, it becomes clear that Japanese mythology is a vital part of the nation's cultural heritage, offering profound wisdom and a window into the collective psyche of its people. It invites us to reflect on our own beliefs and the stories that shape our understanding of the world.

It is my hope that this work has not only informed but also inspired further interest in the fascinating world of Japanese mythology. May these stories continue to be told, reinterpreted, and cherished for generations to come, bridging the gap between the ancient and the modern, the earthly and the divine.

Thank you for your attention to my book!

Arthur Weiss, 2024.

Printed in France by Amazon
Brétigny-sur-Orge, FR

43388012R00073